BIRMINGHAM IN THE FORTIES

Alton & Jo Douglas

The Onion Fair, under construction, Serpentine Ground, Aston, 28th September 1949.

1

© 2000 Alton and Jo Douglas
ISBN 1 85858 171 0
Published by Brewin Books Ltd., Doric House, 56 Alcester Road, Studley, Warwickshire B80 7LG.
Printed by Warwick Printing Co. Ltd., Theatre Street, Warwick CV34 4DR.
Layout by Alton and Jo Douglas

Preparations are underway for the Royal visit the following week, Council House, 8th May 1948.

Front Cover: The official last tram, on the Ladywood route, waits to pull out from Navigation Street,
1st September 1947.

Contents

BREWIN BOOKS LTD

Doric House, 56 Alcester Road,
Studley, Warwickshire B80 7LG

Tel: 01527 854228 Fax: 01527 852746

Vat Registration No. 705 0077 73

Dear Nostalgic,

One little niggle, at the back of my mind, when we set out on this adventure was that, having produced three books on the city during the Second World War, ("Birmingham at War Vol 1", "Birmingham at War Vol 2" and "Birmingham: The War Years") and several titles that included items from those eventful years, there might be a shortage of material. I reckoned, foolishly, without your help – in the end we finished up with enough rare items to fill the deepest bomb crater! So, in your hands, you now have a scrapbook packed to the gunnels (that's quite enough wartime images for one brief intro!) with material that takes us up to the end of the war and then into those difficult, challenging years that lay immediately afterwards. Has there ever been such an engrossing period in our city's history? I think not.

Yours, in friendship,

Alton

Digbeth, 26th June 1949.

1940

Keys make salvage

Birmingham has begun a drive for old, unwanted keys for salvage.

Stacking aluminium pots and pans, for use in the manufacture of fighter planes, 1940.

Grub up!-An Anti-Aircraft Station, c 1940.

BOXING

TOWER BALLROOM
GALALAND,   EDGBASTON
BIRMINGHAM.

MONDAY EVENING, MARCH, 4th, 1940
(FULL MOON)
DOORS OPEN 7 O'CLOCK.   SHOW STARTS 7-45 PROMPT.

JACK INCLEY presents
GREAT SENSATIONAL TEN (2-MIN.) ROUNDS MIDDLEWEIGHT
CONTEST

DICK TURPIN
LEAMINGTON. This great 18-year Coloured Lad is undoubtedly the greatest middleweight discovery for years. Has defeated Johnny Bate (Worcester), Alf. Bishop (West of England Champion), Jack McKnight (Irish Middleweight Champion), Charlie Parkin (Northern Area Champion), Wally Pack (ex-A.B.A. Champion), Maurice Dennis (ex-A.B.A. Champion and Golden Gloves winner), Ben Valentine (Fiji Isles Champion, twice points. V.

SERGT.-INSTRUCTOR
DAVE McCLEAVE
LONDON. (Ex-Welterweight Champion of Great Britain). Won Southern Area Welterweight Title by defeating Ginger Sadd, pts. Won vacant Welterweight Championship by defeating Chuck Parker, has also defeated Jack Lord, 5 rounds, Johnny Rust, 5 Rounds, Dai Farmer Jones, points, Paul Schaefer, points, Jack Powell, 2 Rounds, Freddie Mills, points, Charlie Parkin, 4 Rounds. Lost Welterweight Title to Jake Kilrain, owing to weight difficulties, now chief contender for Middleweight Title.

OPENING SIX (2-MIN.) ROUNDS CONTEST
JIM BOYCE v. CHARLIE WOODS
(COVENTRY)   (NORTHAMPTON).

SMASHING TEN (3-MIN.) ROUNDS FLYWEIGHT CONTEST
FRANK (KID) BONSOR
NOTTINGHAM. Flyweight Champion of the Midlands. Winner of Certificate of Merit. The only British Boxer to stop Jimmy Warnock. Has defeated Harry Orton, Billy Nash, Walter Morton, Dick Lewis, the only boxer in the World to defeat Jimmy Webster, Fly and Bantamweight Champion of South Africa. V.

SAMMY REYNOLDS
WOLVERHAMPTON. Won 26 out of 29 fights by the k.o. Defeated Eric Jones (Southern Area Champion), Pat Mac Stravick, Alex Knight (South African Champion), Sid Parkin, Joe Curran (Liverpool). This is Reynolds' greatest fight to date.

SPECIAL EIGHT (2-MIN.) ROUNDS CONTEST
Billy HOPE v. Jack ROGERS
(NORTHAMPTON)   (WILLENHALL)

GRAND TEN (3-MIN.) ROUNDS RETURN LIGHTWEIGHT CONTEST
ALF. EDWARDS
(SMETHWICK)   V.
JIM WELLARD
(NORTHAMPTON)
When these lads met at last show it looked like developing into a great fight, when Edwards was disqualified for an alleged low blow. Both boys are very confident of victory.

All Officials Licensed by the B.B.B. of C.

Popular Prices : Reserved Ringside 5/6 & 3/6 : Seats Unreserved 2/6 ; Standing 1/6.
Tickets obtainable from Mr. Tom Murphy, "Farcroft Hotel," Rookery Road, Handsworth. Phone—Northern 0957 ; Mr. D. W. Davies, Barrow Street, West Bromwich, Phone—W.B. 0450 ; Mr. Ernest Boynton, "Wagon and Horses" Hotel, Edgbaston St., Phone—Midland 2397 ; Galaland Reservoir, Edgbaston 0135.

Dignitaries at the opening of the Maternity and Child Welfare Centre, Tower Hill, Perry Barr, 5th March 1940.

Local Defence Volunteers (shortly to become the Home Guard) shoulder arms, May 1940.

A gas-proof kennel, 1940.

ARP (Air Raid Precaution) Wardens, May 1940.

CITY OF BIRMINGHAM

AIR RAID PRECAUTIONS

AIR RAID WARDENS SERVICE

1. Volunteers, both male and female, are needed under the Air Raid Precautions Scheme to carry out the duties of Air Raid Wardens, and an outline of these duties and of the training required is given below.

2. It is most essential that this training, which includes a course of instruction in anti-gas measures, be undertaken in peace time since it would not be possible to acquire a useful degree of knowledge in the very short period of time available between the first condition of a state of international tension and the probable occurrence of air raids with or without any formal declaration of war.

DUTIES

3. An Air Raid Warden should regard himself or herself as a member of the general public, chosen and trained to be a leader of his or her fellow citizens, and with them and for them to do the right thing in an emergency. The keynotes of a warden's conduct should be courage and presence of mind.

4. The principal duties may be divided into those to be carried out in time of peace, those to be undertaken immediately prior to the outbreak of hostilities, and those to be undertaken in time of war.

A. DUTIES IN TIME OF PEACE
   (i) Becoming fully trained as an air raid warden and acquiring a detailed knowledge of the local authorities air raid precautions organization.
   (ii) Learning all about the sector, consisting of a street, or streets, to which he or she is posted, noting the location of fire hydrants and telephones, and acquiring a knowledge of his or her neighbours and particularly of those who could be relied upon for assistance in an emergency.
   (iii) Carrying out a census of persons within a sector for the purpose of fitting them with respirators and noting respirator requirements.
   (iv) Assisting members of the general public with advice and guidance.

B. DUTIES IMMEDIATELY PRIOR TO THE OUTBREAK OF HOSTILITIES
   (i) Issuing respirators to the civil population.
   (ii) Assisting members of the general public with help and advice in making their own precautions as good and efficient as possible.

C. DUTIES IN WAR TIME
   ON THE AIR RAID WARNING SIGNAL BEING GIVEN
   (i) Assisting the police in clearing the streets and shepherding into public shelters those individuals who have been caught away from their own homes.
   (ii) PREVENTING PANIC AMONG CIVILIANS, particularly in setting an example by his or her own calm behaviour.

   AFTER THE RAID IS OVER
   (iii) The one duty of paramount importance at this time is to report all damage, the resulting casualties, if any, and the presence or absence of gas within the sector to the Report Centre.
   (iv) Otherwise dealing with the situation in places where bombs have fallen on the lines indicated in A. R. P. Handbook No. 8, " The Duties of a Warden," with which, of course, the warden must be familiar.

PUBLIC NOTICES

YOU MUST USE YOUR OWN SHELTER

PUBLIC SHELTERS
are intended to provide accommodation for people caught in the street during air raids. Sufficient have been built for any likely number.

SHELTER AT HOME
has been provided for a million people.

If you leave your own shelter and go to a public one, you take up the accommodation of people for whom it was made.

THAT MUST NOT HAPPEN
Only if you have no shelter can you be permitted to use a public one at night. Even then, it is better to arrange for your own protection at home.

YOU MAY NOT TAKE INTO A SHELTER
Furniture, perambulators, or anything likely to cause obstruction

If you leave any property behind after a raid it will be put out side, and the Corporation cannot accept responsibility for it

THERE CAN BE NO RESERVED SEATS
You must take away everything you bring in, and you must restrict what you bring in to that which is absolutely necessary

YOU MUST NOT SMOKE IN A SHELTER
It is dangerous. If you really need one, go outside and come back later.

YOU MUST NOT COMMIT A NUISANCE YOURSELF
and if anyone else disturbs order in a shelter, call the Police Such persons will be dealt with as they deserve.

BEST OF ALL — USE YOUR ANDERSON AND STOP AT HOME

If you can act as a Shelter Marshal, send in your name.

If you have any old benches suitable for seats, the Shelter Department would be glad of them. Write your offer of help to the Air Raid Precautions Department, 19, Broad Street, Birmingham, 1.

Austin Street, Nechells, 1940.

TILES BROKEN & DISPLACED BY BLAST

GARAGE & SHEDS COMPLETELY WRECKED

ALL WINDOWS SHATTERED

ANDERSON SHELTER INTACT & OCCUPANTS UNHURT THOUGH NEARER TO BOMB THAN HOUSES

CRATER MADE BY MEDIUM BOMB

SPORT can generally find the best answer to the Dismal Jimmies of the world. In a letter to the "Times" Mr. Victor Hely-Hutchinson, writing from Birmingham, says : "I believe that the following true story accurately represents the spirit of England at the moment.

"Yesterday evening the landlord of a public-house in Birmingham observed to a workman, whom he was serving with a drink, that the war news was pretty bad.' 'Oh, I don't know, was the answer, 'after all, it's the final, and we're playing it on our home ground.'"

RESIGNATION OF MR. CHAMBERLAIN. Confidence in the Government led by Mr. Chamberlain was seriously undermined by the general conduct of the war, and after a debate on the question in the Commons on 8 May, Mr. Chamberlain invited the Opposition to serve under him in a reconstructed Cabinet. Labour, however, refused and on 10 May the Premier resigned and was succeeded by Mr. Winston Churchill. Above is seen the new Premier together with some of the new Ministers. The new War Cabinet consisted of the Premier, who also became Minister of Defence; Mr. Chamberlain, Lord President of the Council; Lord Halifax, Foreign Secretary; Mr. C. R. Attlee, Lord Privy Seal, and Mr. Arthur Greenwood, Minister without Portfolio. Other Ministers were: Mr. A. V. Alexander, Admiralty; Mr. Anthony Eden, War; Sir Archibald Sinclair, Air; Sir John Simon, Lord Chancellor; Sir Kingsley Wood, Exchequer; Sir John Anderson, Home Secretary; Lord Lloyd, Colonies; Sir Andrew Duncan, Board of Trade; Mr. Herbert Morrison, Supply; Mr. Duff Cooper, Information; Mr. Ernest Bevin, Labour and National Service; Mr. L. S. Amery, India and Burma; Mr. Malcolm MacDonald, Health; Lord Woolton, Food; Viscount Caldicote, Dominions; Mr. Ernest Brown, Scotland; Lord Beaverbrook, Aircraft Production; Mr. H. Ramsbotham, Education; Mr. Robert Hudson, Agriculture; Sir John Reith, Transport; Mr. Ronald Cross, Shipping, and Mr. Hugh Dalton, Economic Warfare.

Mr. Chamberlain in a broadcast after his resignation of the Premiership:

Early this morning, without warning or excuse, Hitler added another to the horrible crimes which already disgrace his name by a sudden attack on Holland, Belgium and Luxembourg. In all history no other man has been responsible for such a hideous toll of human suffering and misery as he.

He has chosen a moment when perhaps it seemed to him that this country was entangled in the throes of a political crisis, and when he might find it divided against itself. If he has counted on our internal divisions to help him, he has miscalculated the minds of this people. . . .

The hour has come when we are to be put to the test, as the innocent people of Holland and Belgium and France are being tested already and you and I must rally behind our new leader, and with our united strength and with unshakable courage fight and work until this wild beast that has sprung out of his lair upon us is finally disarmed and overthrown.

OUR SKIPPER

We shall never Surrender

EVEN though large tracts of Europe and many old and famous states have fallen or may fall into the grip of the Gestapo, and all the odious apparatus of Nazi rule, we shall not flag or fail. We shall go on to the end; we shall fight . . . on the seas and oceans; we shall fight with growing confidence and growing strength in the air; we shall defend our island whatever the cost may be. We shall fight on the beaches; we shall fight on the landing grounds; we shall fight in the fields and in the streets; we shall fight in the hills. We shall never surrender.

Extract from Prime Minister's Speech of June 4, 1940.

There is a curious postscript to what is possibly the most famous speech in history. It is an established fact that Churchill actually delivered the speech himself, in the House of Commons. However, in 1979, the actor, Norman Shelley, claimed that, because the new Prime Minister was very busy and he was known for his impression of him, his voice was heard on the historic broadcast, later in the day, not Churchill's!

AIR RAID WARNINGS

Warning of impending air raids will be given by a fluctuating or "warbling" signal of varying pitch, or a succession of intermittent blasts sounded by hooters and sirens.

These signals may be supplemented by sharp blasts on police whistles.

The "RAIDERS PASSED" signal will be a continuous signal at a steady pitch.

IF POISON GAS has been used, warning will be given by HAND RATTLES. The ringing of HAND BELLS will announce that the danger from gas has passed.

Every householder, or head of a family or business, should learn now how to protect, in war-time, his own people and home from the effects of explosive bombs, incendiary bombs, and poison gas.

Sandbags, to protect against bomb blast, around the main entrance to the Law Courts, Corporation Street, c 1940.

Belvedere Road, Erdington, 1940.

If the
INVADER
comes

WHAT TO DO — AND HOW TO DO IT

THE Germans threaten to invade Great Britain. If they do so they will be driven out by our Navy, our Army and our Air Force. Yet the ordinary men and women of the civilian population will also have their part to play. Hitler's invasions of Poland, Holland and Belgium were greatly helped by the fact that the civilian population was taken by surprise. They did not know what to do when the moment came. *You must not be taken by surprise.* This leaflet tells you what general line you should take. More detailed instructions will be given you when the danger comes nearer. Meanwhile, read these instructions carefully and be prepared to carry them out.

I

When Holland and Belgium were invaded, the civilian population fled from their homes. They crowded on the roads, in cars, in carts, on bicycles and on foot, and so helped the enemy by preventing their own armies from advancing against the invaders. You must not allow that to happen here. Your first rule, therefore, is :—

(1) IF THE GERMANS COME, BY PARACHUTE, AEROPLANE OR SHIP, YOU MUST REMAIN WHERE YOU ARE. THE ORDER IS " STAY PUT ".

If the Commander in Chief decides that the place where you live must be evacuated, he will tell you when and how to leave. Until you receive such orders you must remain where you are. If you run away, you will be exposed to far greater danger because you will be machine-gunned from the air as were civilians in Holland and Belgium, and you will also block the roads by which our own armies will advance to turn the Germans out.

II

There is another method which the Germans adopt in their invasion. They make use of the civilian population in order to create confusion and panic. They spread false rumours and issue false instructions. In order to prevent this, you should obey the second rule, which is as follows :—

(2) DO NOT BELIEVE RUMOURS AND DO NOT SPREAD THEM. WHEN YOU RECEIVE AN ORDER, MAKE QUITE SURE THAT IT IS A TRUE ORDER AND NOT A FAKED ORDER. MOST OF YOU KNOW YOUR POLICEMEN AND YOUR A.R.P. WARDENS BY SIGHT, YOU CAN TRUST THEM. IF YOU KEEP YOUR HEADS, YOU CAN ALSO TELL WHETHER A MILITARY OFFICER IS REALLY BRITISH OR ONLY PRETENDING TO BE SO. IF IN DOUBT ASK THE POLICE-MAN OR THE A.R.P. WARDEN. USE YOUR COMMON SENSE.

Special Warnings To Workers

A scheme to give factory workers a special air-raid warning to avoid unnecessary interruption of production was discussed yesterday in London by the T.U.C.

The plan, drawn up by the Ministry of Home Security, Air Ministry, Unions and Employers' organisations, is based on a system of roof-watchers and look-out men who will give warnings only if it is really necessary.

BRITAIN SEIZES THE FRENCH FLEET
Ministry of Information Statement, July 4, 1940

It will be recalled that the French Government, relying upon the promises of Germany and Italy not to use her Fleet against France's former Ally, undertook by the terms of the armistice to allow their Fleet to pass into the hands of the enemy.

His Majesty's Government, having lost all faith in promises made by the Governments of Germany and Italy, felt that they were compelled, not only in their own interests, but also in the hope of restoring the independence of France and the integrity of the French Empire, to take steps to ensure that the French Fleet should not be used against them by the common enemy.

With this object in view steps were taken in the early morning of July 3 to place all French men-of-war in British ports under British control.

At the same time French vessels in ports of North Africa were offered certain conditions designed solely for the purpose of keeping them out of German hands.

It was explained to the officer in command that if none of these conditions were accepted Great Britain was prepared to take every step in order to ensure that none of these vessels should be used against her.

His Majesty's Government deeply regret that the French admiral in command at Oran refused to accept any of the conditions proposed, with the inevitable result that action had to be taken.

THE LORD MAYOR of Birmingham on Wednesday appealed for gifts binoculars for the use of the Army. His appeal was urgent as many binoculars were lost in the withdrawal of the B.E.F. from France. The Lord Mayor arranged to receive gifts at the Council House at noon yesterday and by half-past twelve thirty-seven pairs had been handed in. Later gifts raised the total to fifty.

More rifle drill for the Home Guard,
23rd September 1940.

The interior of The Empire Theatre,
Smallbrook Street/Hurst Street, October 1940.

The result of a direct hit on the Wesleyan and General Assurance Society, Steelhouse Lane, 26th October 1940.

Police investigate big factory fire

Police are investigating the cause of a fire which destroyed a Birmingham factory yesterday. The outbreak was discovered about an hour and a half after the employees had left.

Firemen were hampered by white-hot metal which spread in all directions. Several minor explosions threw clouds of sparks high in the air.

Woodbridge Road, Moseley, October 1940.

Petrol Up To 1s. 9½d. Today

THE price of pool motor spirit is raised today by 1½d. a gallon to 1s. 9½d.—the highest price for 15 years—with the usual surcharges for North and West Scotland, etc. The Government has agreed to the increase, which follows an earlier rise of 2d. a gallon made on October 17.

FIFTY THOUSAND radio sets, now installed in motor-cars in Great Britain, will have to be dismantled soon and removed.

A new Emergency Powers (Defence) Regulation, issued by the Postmaster-General yesterday says: "No person shall use or have in his possession or under his control any radio receiving apparatus installed in any road vehicle."

The carrying of portable radio sets in cars is also forbidden. For the purposes of this regulation a radio set is deemed to be installed, even if it is not fixed in position, "in circumstances in which it can be readily adapted for use."

The exact date on which car radios must be dismantled is not fixed.

LEMONS are unobtainable in Birmingham. This is by no means surprising since Italy and Spain are the source of the supply.

"I haven't a lemon in the shop," confessed a fruiterer today, "and I don't give much for your chance of getting any. There may be a few during the next day or two, when a ship comes in, but the scarcity is certain to continue."

English apples may be had in a wide range, with Worcester Pearmains popular at 8d. to 10d. per lb. Imported apples are costing 10d. per lb. and cookers 3d. to 4d. Cultivated blackberries are available at 1s. per lb. Oranges are from 2s. to 3s. per dozen, according to size, and grapefruit 6d. each.

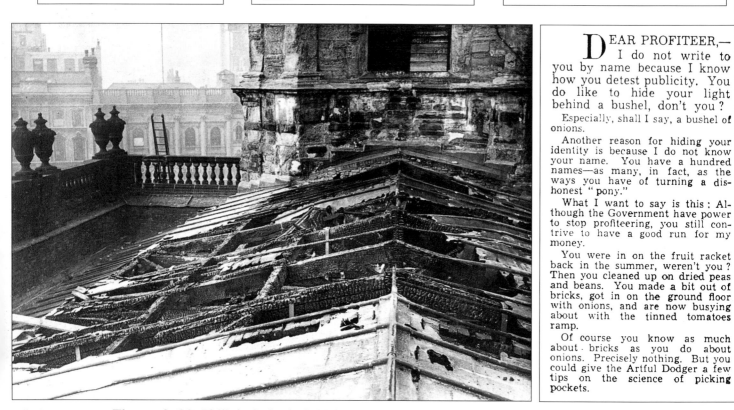

The roof of St Philip's Cathedral, 29th October 1940.

DEAR PROFITEER,— I do not write to you by name because I know how you detest publicity. You do like to hide your light behind a bushel, don't you?

Especially, shall I say, a bushel of onions.

Another reason for hiding your identity is because I do not know your name. You have a hundred names—as many, in fact, as the ways you have of turning a dishonest " pony."

What I want to say is this : Although the Government have power to stop profiteering, you still contrive to have a good run for my money.

You were in on the fruit racket back in the summer, weren't you ? Then you cleaned up on dried peas and beans. You made a bit out of bricks, got in on the ground floor with onions, and are now busying about with the tinned tomatoes ramp.

Of course you know as much about bricks as you do about onions. Precisely nothing. But you could give the Artful Dodger a few tips on the science of picking pockets.

ALL ROUND ECONOMY

To make tea go much farther put a quarter of a pound of tea in the oven for ten or fifteen minutes or until well dry. Then put it between the folds of a newspaper and crush with a rolling-pin. You will be surprised to find how much further it goes.—J. Davison.

To save gas or other fuel when making a suet pudding, whether meat or fruit, cut a small piece of the suet paste about the size of a penny from the bottom of the paste. Then fill up the basin, and cover with a round of paste as usual, and the pudding will take much less time to cook, as the heat can get through the centre of the pudding immediately.—Mrs. B. N. Hughes.

Some people cannot wear Wellington boots because of the rubber being cold to their feet. A good way to avoid this is by making use of an old pair of fur-lined gauntlet gloves. Take out the fur and get a pair of socks the required size of the boot, then gum the skin side of the fur to the socks. These will be found most warm and comfortable.—Miss B. Rigby.

WORK OF THE HOUSE

When oiling wringers, if the bearings are lubricated with glycerine instead of ordinary oil, the clothes will not be marked should they come in contact with it.—Mrs. C. Phillpott.

Round the rim of cake-tins, etc., packed to the men of the Fighting Forces stick adhesive tape. It ensures the lid fitting tightly and keeps the contents airtight.—Mrs. S. John.

To prevent a draining-board rotting that is continually exposed to water make it waterproof in this way. Scrub the board well and allow it to dry, then rub it over with paraffin wax, forcing the wax into the wood by ironing your board with a warm iron.

E.N.S.A. PLANS MORE SHOWS

Plans to double concerts, sports and studies for the Services will be in operation by the autumn.

Six hundred jobless actors and actresses will help E.N.S.A. to give every soldier at least one show a fortnight.

Bigger libraries, lectures by schoolmasters and professors of first-class qualifications, optional lessons for all ranks, will, it is hoped, cater for every soldier.

Butter Ration Cut Two Ounces

The butter allowance is to be reduced from 6oz. to 4oz. from Monday next.

"This only affects people who have been in the habit of taking all their 6oz. ration in butter," a Food Ministry official said. "People who have normally drawn all their ration—6oz.—in margarine will not be affected."

---

17 DOWN

SEVENTEEN German aircraft were shot down in raids over this country yesterday. One of our fighters was lost.

Tindal Street School, Cromer Road, Balsall Heath, October 1940.

Holloway Head, October 1940.

The once-splendid dining room of the Great Western Hotel, at Snow Hill Station, November 1940.

Good Health!

For her Children's Sake— the wise Mother insists on

WATHES, CATTELL & GURDEN, LTD., BIRMINGHAM, 4.

GOVERNMENT EVACUATION SCHEME

The Government have ordered evacuation of registered school children.

If your children are registered, visit their assembly point at once and read the instructions on the notice board.

The name and address of the assembly point is given on the notice to parents.

Posters notifying arrival will be displayed at the schools at which the children assemble for evacuation.

Thank you, Foster-Parents ... we want more like you!

Some kindly folk have been looking after children from the cities for over six months. Extra work? Yes, they've been a handful!... but the foster-parents know they have done the right thing.

And think of all the people who have cause to be thanking the foster-parents. First, the children themselves. They're out of a danger-zone — where desperate peril may come at any minute. And they're healthier and happier. Perhaps they don't say it but they certainly mean "Thank you".

Then their parents. Think what it means to them!

The Government are grateful to all the 20,000 people in Scotland who are so greatly helping the country by looking after evacuated children. But many new volunteers are needed—to share in the present task and to be ready for any crisis that may come. Won't you be one of them? All you need do is enrol your name with the local Authority. You will be doing a real service for the nation. You may be saving a child's life.

The Secretary of State, who has been entrusted by the Government with the conduct of evacuation, asks you urgently to join the Roll of those who are willing to receive children. Please apply to your local Council.

Boarding school children who are usually given a half-term holiday so that they can get home will be disappointed this year. The Government, it was stated yesterday, hopes that schools will dispense with this holiday this year.

Evacuation time for pupils from St Chad's Roman Catholic School, Shadwell Street, at Snow Hill Station, c1940.

Queen Street/Highgate Road, 20th November 1940.

Moseley, November 1940.

From John Bright Street, looking towards New Street Station, 21st November 1940

The junction of Gooch Street and Bromsgrove Street, 21st November 1940.

Great Western Arcade, 25th November 1940.

The King visits Aston, 13th December 1940.

Carols, played by the Salvation Army Band, in the Minories (facing Bull Street), 24th December 1940.

Swanshurst Lane, Moseley, January 1941.

COAL hoarders may have their stocks seized : eggs —at last—are more plentiful : face powders and creams may soon be obtainable for a time : razor blades are to be still scarcer.

Such is to-day's News From the Home Front.

Alfred Road, Sparkhill, 2nd January 1941.

WOMEN WANTED
to take over the
BALLOON BARRAGE

The nightmare of Nazi airmen is Britain's balloon barrage. That's why it is one of the most important jobs in the country to keep those silver fish flying! And the WAAF have proved they can take over this important front-line job from the RAF!

It's a fine, healthy life for women who are fit and strong and fond of the open air. You must be 5' 1" or over, and aged between 17½ and 43. After a short training course, you will be posted to a balloon site. Sites are usually in or near a town. There you will live and work in a small community of about a dozen or so. When fully trained your minimum pay is 3/- a day *and all found.*

In addition to balloon operation, there are many other interesting trades open now in the WAAF. Every woman not doing vital work is asked to volunteer.

A Serviceman's wife does NOT lose her allowance on joining up, and she IS granted her leave to coincide with her husband's leave, subject only to urgent Service considerations.

Go to a Recruiting Centre* or Employment Exchange for fuller information. If you are in work, *they* will find out whether you can be spared from it. If you cannot go at once, send in the coupon.

When this girl joined the WAAF six months ago, to become a balloon operator, she was badly under weight. Now she's back to normal. "You can tell them from me, it's a grand life!" she says.

*Single girls born between January 1st, 1918, and June 30th, 1922, come under the National Service Act and *must* go to the Employment Exchange, *not* a Recruiting Centre.

WAAF

297 Oxford Street, London, W.1   3010   *AR 10*

Please send me full information about the trade of Balloon Operator in the WAAF.

Mrs. ⎱
Miss ⎰ _____   *Cross out " Mrs." or " Miss "*

Address _____

County_____ Date of birth_____ *In confidence*

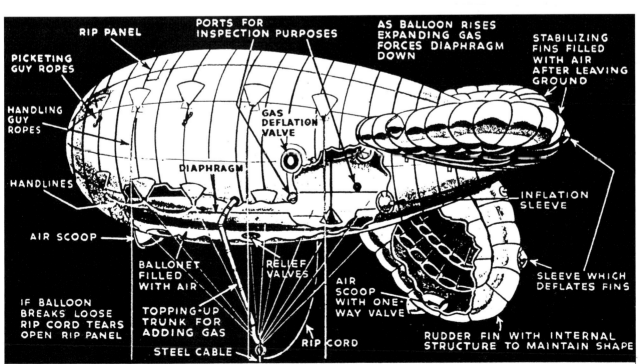

Showing the constructional details of a British barrage balloon. Fear of collision with the balloon or its trailing steel cable compels enemy bombers to fly high, where they are more vulnerable to our A.A. fire and less able to bomb with precision. The balloons cost about £100 each to construct. The gas for each filling costs about £25.

We could lose the
war by Fire!
Be ready for
FIREBOMB FRITZ

The balloon barrage which effectively stops enemy dive bombers from
approaching their targets, 1941.

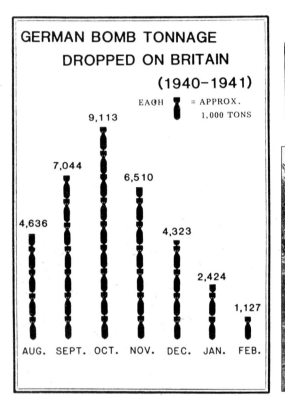

GERMAN BOMB TONNAGE
DROPPED ON BRITAIN
(1940–1941)

EACH = APPROX. 1,000 TONS

AUG.	SEPT.	OCT.	NOV.	DEC.	JAN.	FEB.
4,636	7,044	9,113	6,510	4,323	2,424	1,127

The Home Guard protect a German plane downed in Pype Hayes Park,
1941.

"Made in Germany, finished in England!" A wartime slogan that sums up the feeling at the time, 1941.

A new protective helmet for roof spotters, 1941. Unfortunately, it was made of asbestos!

Home Guard Parade marching down Colmore Row into Victoria Square, 23rd March 1941.

The premises of W.H. Smart & Co. Ltd., (ham and bacon curers), Birmingham Ham Market, Wrentham Street, 9th April 1941.

The Lord Mayor, Ald. Wilfrid Martineau, before acting as chairman at the re-opening of the Methodist Youth Club, with some of the guests, Perry Common Community Hall, 10th March 1941.

SHOP GIRLS, typists, dressmakers, usherettes —all girls, in fact, who have been thrown out of their normal employment by the war—are invited to sign on for war work at their local Labour Exchanges on Monday.

On this day the great drive begins to get 500,000 extra women into war industry. Officials will be ready with all the answers to the hundred and one questions the women will want to ask.

Who will look after my baby? How will I get to and from work? What will I be paid when trained? How do I live till then? Will you find me a job at the end of the training? And so on.

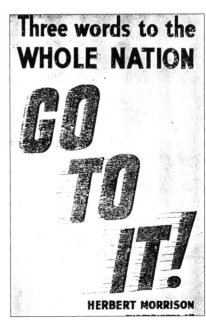

Three words to the WHOLE NATION

GO TO IT!

HERBERT MORRISON

Nechells Green, 15th April 1941.

The Dinner Hour Service, conducted by Canon Guy
Rogers, St Martin's, 17th April 1941.

St. Martin's, 1941.

AERIAL BOMBARDMENT
Emergency Rest Centres

Persons whose houses have been destroyed or damaged by Enemy Action and who are
temporarily homeless may be accommodated in **REST CENTRES** until other
arrangements are made; similarly the **REST CENTRES** are available for
persons who have left their homes by reason of the proximity of Unexploded Bombs

CONVOY YOUR **COUNTRY** TO **VICTORY**
SAVE AND **LEND**
THROUGH OUR
NATIONAL SAVINGS GROUP

PICTURE FANS.

A for Anna Neagle who sings like a bird,
B for Boris Karloff who makes me feel scared,
C for Clark Gable who sends girls' hearts a-flutter,
D for David Niven who makes us all stutter.
E for Eleanor Powell who looks glamorous at nights,
F for Fred Astaire who dances in tights.
G for Gordon Harker whose voice sounds like thunder,
H for Hedy Lammar whose spell all men fall under.
I for Irene Dunn who makes love look exciting,
J for James Cagney who loves to be fighting.
K for Katherine Hepburn who's got a cute figure,
L for Lana Turner who's quite a gold digger.
M for Mickey Rooney who's always in trouble,
N for Ned Sparks who can knock back a double.
O for Oliver Hardy who's fair, fat and forty,
P for Pat Kirkwood who's inclined to be naughty.
Q for Queenie the dog we all fall for,
R for Robert Taylor the guy girls leave home for.
S for Spencer Tracy whose acting is terrific,
T for Tyrone Power who cruises the Pacific.
U for Una Merkel who acts quite the lady,
V for Victor Maclagan who'd look good in the Navy.
W for Will Hay (makes us think of D.C.S.),
X for (beats me, I'll leave you to guess).
Y for Yvonne who designs all the gowns
Z for Zeigfield Girls who banish men's frowns.

Brook Hill Road, Ward End, 28th April 1941.

Inside Information!

Edgbaston Street, showing Lease Lane (with the Market Hall at the top) and the Waggon & Horses (right), April 1941.

Addison Road, Nechells, 1941.

Newton Street, devastation after the night of 9th April 1941.

A job interview being conducted at a Birmingham Labour Exchange, 19th May 1941.

A female porter at New Street Station, 1941.

NATIONAL SERVICE (ARMED FORCES) ACTS

GRADE CARD.

Registration No. *Bxx 22929*

Mr. *Percival J Lockwood*

whose address on his registration card is ....

21 Heath Green Rd B'ham 18.

was medically examined at **BIRMINGHAM MEDICAL BOARD (No.2)**

on *20 MAY 1941*

and placed in

GRADE* ....

E.D. Until* .... (Medical Board stamp.)

Chairman of Board ....

Man's Signature *P. T. Lockwood.*

*The roman numeral denoting the man's Grade (with number also spelt out) will be entered in RED ink by the Chairman himself, e.g., Grade I (one), Grade II (two) (a) (Vision). If the examination is deferred the Chairman will enter a date after the words "E.D. Until", and cross out "Grade"; alternatively, the words "E.D. Until............" will be struck out.

N.S. 55

Bankes Road, Small Heath, July 1941. Note the bedroom windows, on the left, have been blast-proofed.

M. A. LLOYD & SON Ltd.

DIRECTORS: L. A. LLOYD, S. C. LLOYD, H. L. LLOYD

TELEGRAMS: "INKSTAND," BIRMINGHAM
TELEPHONE: ASTON CROSS 1468

MANUFACTURERS OF
STATIONERS' SUNDRIES
AND
LADIES' HAND BAG FRAMES & FITTINGS
ALSO
ACCURATE PRESSED & MACHINED WORK

CONTRACTORS TO H.M. HOME AND COLONIAL GOVERNMENTS

PRINCIP St., BIRMINGHAM, 4

21st May, 1941.

The Manager,
    Ministry of Labour & National Service,
      Employment Exchange,
        281, Corporation Street,
        BIRMINGHAM.

Dear Sir,

      Re - Percival T. Lockwood,
      21, Heath Green Road, B'ham.18.

    You have our application for Registration under the Protected Establishments on account of the Ministry of Aircraft Production.

    We have been busy for the last six months making tools and getting ready for production of the 20 m.m. Hispano Cartridge Link. We started production only two months ago, and are now turning out 30/40,000 a week.

    Owing to the big change over, we have lost a lot of our labour during the last six months. Now the Ministry of Aircraft Production are pressing us to increase our output to 100,000 a week, so that you will see that we cannot part with the labour we have, as we find it exceedingly difficult to get any fresh work people.

    Although Percy Lockwood is registered as a Cabinet Maker, we now use him as our maintenance hand, and are relying upon his services to help increase our production.

              We are,
              Yours faithfully,
        for M. A. LLOYD & SON, LTD.

The Lord Mayor, Ald. Wilfrid Martineau (centre), takes part in a broadcast, 4th July 1941.

Millward Street, Bordesley, July 1941.

Millward Street, Bordesley, July 1941.

WHY AREN'T THERE MORE TRAINS?

Factories turning out guns, bombers and fighters depend on the Railways for supplies.

To keep them working at top pressure the Railways must run thousands of additional goods trains by day and night.

The Railways must also keep the Nation's food, coal and export trades moving.

Essential trains must have first claim on the lines. *It is as vital to ration trains as it is to ration food.* The Railways are giving you every passenger train the tracks will take.

WE'LL BEAT HITLER BY HELPING ONE ANOTHER

BRITISH RAILWAYS

Handsworth Home Guard, with Frank Broom (the Aston Villa and England footballer), sitting second left, 1941.

Army manoeuvres in Pinfold Street, July 1941. This group was captured – fortunately it was not for real!

The mounted Home Guard awaits orders, Sutton Park, 7th July 1941.

Birmingham evacuees, hop-picking in Worcester during the school holidays, September 1941.

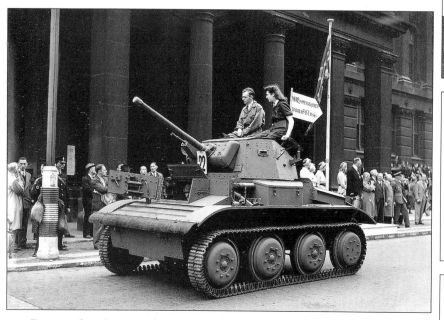

Due to the shortage of men, more women are needed in heavy industry, 1941.

A recruiting parade, outside the Council House, September 1941.

Carroty George

He's a great favourite in the kitchen, our Carroty George. He has a hundred and one ways of making himself agreeable. Given a chance he'll enter into your pots and pans with real relish. Even if you reduce him to dice he won't be cut up; and he takes frying, steaming, stewing or boiling, in perfectly good part. He plays the leading part in

Club Carrots

Scrub and grate six large carrots and mix with a teaspoonful of finely shredded white heart of cabbage. Make a dressing of 1 small teacupful thick unflavoured custard, 1 tablespoon salad oil, 1 teaspoon vinegar, ½ teaspoon each mustard, pepper, and salt, and 1 tablespoon finely chopped pickles. Toast 4 thick slices of bread on each side, then slit open to make large pockets. Spread the insides of these pockets with margarine, and stuff with the filling. Serve at once. A first-rate supper dish.

C6

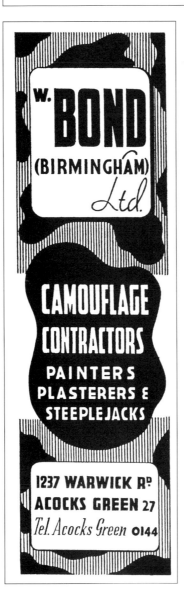

W. BOND (BIRMINGHAM) Ltd.

CAMOUFLAGE CONTRACTORS

PAINTERS PLASTERERS & STEEPLEJACKS

1237 WARWICK Rᵈ ACOCKS GREEN 27

Tel. Acocks Green 0144

WVS (Women's Voluntary Service) workers manage a field kitchen, part of one of the emergency food convoys rushed in to help in bombed areas, c 1941.

The Lord Mayor, Ald. Norman Tiptaft, receives a presentation from Canada,
6th January 1942.

When walking
after dark to-nigh
For safety's sake
wear somethin
WHITE

For the pedestrian: Rememb
that when you can see t
motorist the motorist probab
can't see you. So wear or car
something white or luminous.

For the motorist: Rememb
you are in charge of a weap
that can kill. Be *careful —*
considerate.

★ THERE WERE 1,313 ROA
DEATHS IN DECEMBER-

Ammunition box production, Austin Works, c 1942. This photograph was banned from use until the summer of 194

A Spitfire production line, Castle Bromwich Aeroplane Factory, 1942.

K2 ambulance, made at the Austin Works, Longbridge, c 1942.

THE SUPERMARINE SPITFIRE Mk I

single-seat fighter   Great Britain

THE Supermarine Spitfire single-seat fighter (1,030 h.p. Rolls-Royce Merlin II liquid-cooled motor and D.H. three-blade controllable-pitch airscrew). Low wing cantilever monoplane. Dark brown and green camouflage. Under surfaces: Starboard wing white, port wing black. All-metal construction with stressed metal covering. Eight Browning machine guns, four in each wing, fixed to fire forwards outside airscrew disc. Outwards retracting undercarriage. Fixed tail wheel. Radiator under starboard wing, oil cooler under port wing. Deep breasted nose, elliptical wings. Cantilever fin and rudder. Rounded tailplane.

Span 36 ft. 10 ins. ; length 29 ft. 11 ins. ; height 11 ft. 5 ins. ; wing area 242 sq. ft.   Loaded weight 5,850 lb. Max. speed 387 m.p.h. at 18,500 ft.   Duration 3.6 hours.   Initial climb 2,300 ft. per min.

A lonely plane-spotter at work, c 1942.

A short break from working on aeroplane fuselages, Castle Bromwich Aeroplane Factory, 1942.

Mrs. SEW-and-SEW on

ISSUED BY THE BOARD OF TRADE

Steps you can take to save your SHOES

Buy shoes wisely. Remember that fit is more important than appearance. It's worth a little search to find really comfortable shoes.

New shoes will last longer if worn first on a dry day.

Give your shoes a rest — don't wear the same pair two days running if you can help it.

When you take off your shoes, use shoe-trees or stuff them with paper to keep the shape. Always undo fastenings first.

Damp shoes should be dried out slowly—*never* near strong heat. Put wet "woodies" sole-side up.

Clean regularly — a little polish every time is better than a lot now and then. Use dubbin on boots and shoes for rough wear.

See to repairs promptly — heels especially. A 'run-over' heel spoils the shape of the whole shoe *and* tires the foot. Leather studs and 'rails' on Woodies must be replaced before worn down to the sole.

Rubber studs, rubber soles and iron tips help shoes to wear longer.

* * *

Children's Boots and Shoes
Always buy on the large side to allow for growing. Extra socks will make a slightly big shoe comfortable.

Ask the retailer to advise you which shoes are most durable and suitable for your children

Teach your children to change their shoes on coming indoors.

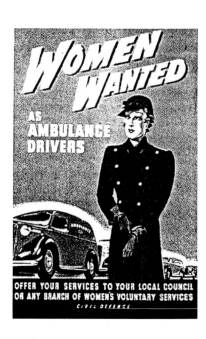
WVS at work in a municipal park, 1942.

King Haakon of Norway (centre in dark coat) inspects a Guard of Honour, Colmore Row, 8th April 1942.

The King and Queen, as part of their endless journey around the British Isles, visit the children of Birchfield Road School, 25th April 1942.

Members of the ATS (Auxiliary Territorial Service, later the WRAC) take a breather, c 1942.

The research team, led by Nobel Prize winner, Professor Sir Norman Haworth (centre), involved in pioneer work for The British Atomic Energy Project, University of Birmingham, c 1942.

CHORUS girls of the touring revues are finding all billets taken by war workers in scores of the smaller manufacturing towns and are having to make shift in their dressing-rooms or among the theatre seats.

Many girls sing and dance with aching backs—the result of sleeping curled up on a "prop" basket.

Almost all the usual theatrical lodgings have been taken by munition workers, evacuees, or the military.

But for all the Alerts, blitzes, and comfortless nights, with perhaps a make-up box for a pillow, the girls carry on cheerfully.

Civil Defence volunteers, Bournbrook, c 1942.

Home Guard under-going anti-aircraft training with rocket projectors, 8th July 1942.

A new device for dealing with incendiary bombs in inaccessible corners, c 1942.

Sparkbrook fire-fighters ready to man the pumps and protect the shops in Stratford Road, c 1942.

Lucas ARP on the roof at Great King Street, Hockley, c 1942.

The Home Secretary, the Rt. Hon. Herbert Morrison (centre), meets fire-fighting chiefs, Central Fire Station, 13th September 1942.

A fire engine and trailer, 1942.

That's just my cup of tea!

The ration that gives more cups of better tea per pot.

LYONS TEA

J. LYONS & COMPANY LTD.

TRAIN TO WIN

APPLY TO THE EMPLOYMENT EXCHANGE
GOVERNMENT TRAINING SCHEMES
WITH PAID ALLOWANCES
100

MINISTRY OF LABOUR AND NATIONAL SERVICE

A COMPLETE BIOGRAPHY OF
LORD HAW-HAW
OF ZEESEN

BY
JONAH BARRINGTON
AND
FENWICK

COVER YOUR HAIR FOR SAFETY

YOUR RUSSIAN SISTER DOES!

Issued by the Ministry of Labour and National Service and produced by the Royal Society for the Prevention of Accidents. Terminal House, 52, Grosvenor Gardens, London, S.W.1.

THURS. 15 OCT
WREN DAY

THE WOMEN'S ROYAL NAVAL SERVICE WANTS VOLUNTEERS
Your chance to learn all about the Service is NEXT THURSDAY

WREN DAY

On this day the W.R.N.S. travelling Interview Officer will be at

Six Ways, Aston, Birmingham.

If you are interested call between 10 a.m. and 5.30 p.m.

Applicants born in the period from January, 1918 to 30th June 1922 inclusive, must apply to their Local Employment Exchange.

WOMEN'S ROYAL NAVAL SERVICE

W.R.N.S.

Lord Dudley about to perform the opening ceremony at the exhibition of paintings from The Tate Gallery. Royal Society of Artists, New Street, 6th November 1942.

1943

High Street, looking towards Dale End,
c 1943.

...bers of the Fire Service, c 1943. It's often forgotten that
...at many women were involved in fire-fighting activities.

...d Woolton, Minister for Food, visits a Birmingham Civic
Restaurant, 26th February 1943.

HINT TO COMPANIES ON A "LONG-OVERDUE REFORM"

"ELECTRIFICATION of the Midland railway systems is long overdue," declared Ald. A. E. Ager, when referring to the problems of reconstruction in his address as chairman at the first annual meeting of the West Midlands Regional Council of the Labour Party, held in Birmingham yesterday.

FOOD FACTS

APPLE HARVEST

Apples are plentiful, and it's grand to serve delicious apple sweets to the family. Eat all you can, revel in apple fool, apple tart, and apple dumpling; but think also of the Winter months ahead when fruit is unobtainable, and *for every pound of apples you eat now preserve another pound for future eating.* Winter meals will prove less of a problem if the larder is stocked with apple pulp, apple rings, apple and ginger jam, and apple chutney. Make the most of the apple harvest.

Apple Pulp

This is a quick and easy way of preserving apples. A large quantity of fruit can be stored in each jar and used later on for making into jam or for making apple puddings.

Peel and core the apples and remove any blemished parts. Stew in a saucepan with just enough water to prevent burning until the fruit is cooked through. While still boiling pour into *hot* bottles and seal immediately with hot lids. When using a screw-band give a half turn back to allow for expansion. Now immerse the bottles in a pan of hot water which must be raised to boiling point and boiled for five minutes. Take out the bottles to cool. Test next day. Remove screw-band or clip: if the seal is perfect it should be possible to lift the jar by the lid. If the lid comes off re-sterilise or use at once. For sweetened pulp follow the method given above, but add a little sugar to the fruit before it is brought to the boil.

Apple Rings

Here's a way of keeping apples that can be used for windfalls or blemished fruit.

Wipe the apples, remove the cores and peel thinly, cutting out any blemishes. Slice into rings about ¼ inch thick. Steep the rings for ten minutes in water containing 1½ oz. of salt to the gallon. Thread the rings on sticks or canes to fit across the oven or spread on trays. Dry very slowly until the rings feel like chamois leather. The temperature should not exceed 150° F. Turn once or twice during drying.

Swiss Apple

This is a quickly-made sweet which the children will love.
Ingredients : 1 large apple, 1 heaped tablespoon rolled oats, 1 heaped teaspoonful sugar, 2 tablespoonfuls evaporated or top milk.
Quantity : one helping.
Method : Soak the rolled oats in the milk for an hour or more. Grate the unpeeled apple and add to the mixture with the sugar. Beat together.

THIS IS WEEK 4—THE LAST WEEK—OF RATION PERIOD No. 1

THE MINISTRY OF FOOD, LONDON, W.I.   FOOD FACTS No. 163

Gas-powered Midland Red Bus, Digbeth, 1943.

Because of the shortage of fuel some city buses were converted to run on gas, produced by burning anthracite. The trailer was then towed behind the bus, c 1943.

Honour Test for Bus Passengers

Instead of a curfew at 9.15 p.m. Birmingham buses will from February 21 run until 10 p.m.

After that time there will be special buses for war workers, and the general public will be put on their honour not to ride in them.

A demolition man checks the steel hawser needed to bring down an unsafe wall, c 1943.

The 49th Bn. Royal Warwickshire Home Guard attack! 1943.

Exercises for the Home Guard, 1943.

NOBLE GIFT BY A BIRMINGHAM MAN

THE Lord Mayor of Birmingham (Councillor W. S. Lewis) announced last night that he had received a wonderful send-off in his effort to raise £60,000 for the R.A.F. Benevolent Fund during his year of office.

Mr. Douglas W. Turner, a well-known Birmingham business man and magistrate, has undertaken to pay £25,000 to the fund by seven yearly instalments

BOMBS on the Axis hour after hour . . . . 8,000-pounders on Pilsen, Essen, Berlin . . . . high-explosives coldly determined by Bomber Command to secure the maximum effect on Nazi armaments and supplies.

Bombs falling precisely and punctually, and, as photographs prove beyond question, hitting the target.

Among the boys who deliver them, twisting and weaving in their Bostons and Lancasters through the treacherous new fields of daisy-flak, there ride ace airmen from the Midlands.

They include 22-year-old veterans like **Erdington's Pilot Officer Bert Meagher**, thrice a visitor to Essen, his D.F.C. scored over Berlin, his D.F.M. won in a trip to Le Creusot

Dress for the Party . . .

We take off 18.50 after briefing. It will be cold in the turrets — Plenty of clothes — three pullovers, roll top sweater, four pairs socks — *Mother would laugh.* Of course I wear 'em plus flying kit gloves and scarf. Now details — revolver, torch, pipe — baccy — thermos, hot coffee, money, clasp knife, matches — extra scarf and gloves!!! *Yes, mother — I'll need 'em all . . . . and then some!* chewing gum, chocolate barley sugar, biscuits, clean rag.

* * * *

I worm myself into the turret, Helmet . . . . Parachute. Plug in the Intercom. Engines tested — Captain asks '*All ready?*' O.K. — We're off to another Party.

* * *

You wouldn't think—would you ?—that so many things were required to put one airman into the fight. Yet so it is—and with every fighting man the same. Thousands of details which must be made and paid for. If you realise this, you will see how much we must work, how much we must save. We cannot work and save too much. SAVE MORE.

. . . ◄ Wings for Victory

"The surest way," Matilda said,
"To give the Axis knocks
Is letting your
        suspenders out
And wearing shorter socks.

The shorter sock saves
        labour, dear.
And tons of precious wool —
Like General Alexander's
        head,
It's practical and cool.

So do not search for
        longer hose —
Forego those extra inches !
With shorter socks
        make Hitler feel
Just where his own shoe
        pinches !"

Wolsey

Stirling bomber production at the Austin Aero Works, c 1943.

RADIO PROGRAMMES

HOME SERVICE

3.0—Band of the East Yorkshire Regiment. 3.30—Evensong. 4.0—Griller String Quartet. 4.45—"Twice-told Tales." 5.0—Welsh programme. 5.30—Children's Hour.

6.0—News; announcements. 6.30—"Mr. Crouper Looks at Life" (No. 6). 6.45—Battersea Grammar School Boys' Band and the Norwich Lads' Club Band. 7.15—Scottish Half-hour. 7.45 — "Youth Must Have Its Swing," with Sid Field and George Black's Youngsters. 8.15—Brains Trust.

9.0—News. 9.25—"British Craftsmen." 9.50 — "Love Behind the Lattice," by Edward Knoblock. 10.20 "My Faith and My Job": Talk. 10.35—Dostoevsky and Turgenev: A study by V. S. Pritchett. 11.15—Philharmonic Harp Trio. 11.35—Victor Silvester's Ballroom Orchestra. 12.0—News.

FOR THE FORCES

3.0—Home. 3.30—The Bob Crosby and Casa Loma Orchestra. 4.0—Felton Rapley (organ). 4.20—Maurice Kasket's Orchestra and Edmundo Ros's Rumba Band. 5.0—B.B.C. Revue Chorus and Orchestra. 5.30—"The Trojans": Berlioz's last opera on records.

6.0—Home.   6.30 — Australian news. 6.40—New Zealand news. 6.50—South African news. 7.0—American Sports news. 7.5—"These You Have Loved": Records. 7.50—B.B.C. Midland Light Orchestra. 8.25—Jack Payne's Orchestra.

9.0—Home. 9.25—"Into Battle." 9.35—"The Music Society of Lower Basin Street" (No. 11). 10.0—"Tuesday Radiogram." 10.30—Harold Collins' Orchestra (recording).

St John the Baptist Church,
Chapel House Street/Deritend,
c 1943.

PARENTS' PETITION

ACCOMMODATION AT STECHFORD ROAD

THREAT TO KEEP CHILDREN AWAY

At a recent meeting of the Birmingham Education Committee a petition was submitted on behalf of the parents of children attending the Stechford Road School and living on the Firs Estate and the Ideal Homes Estate, Castle Bromwich.

They asked the Education Committee to take over from the Public Health Department the existing day nursery at the corner of the Heathway, transfer the children to another day nursery about 200 yards away, then use the first day nursery as an infants' school to relieve Stechford Road School and, meanwhile, erect a temporary infants' school on or near the Firs Estate before next winter.

The petitioners say that if the suggestions are not complied with it is feared there will be serious trouble next winter, as most of the petitioners are not prepared to send their children to school in bad weather.

NOT SUITABLE FOR FAMILY LIFE

Flats are condemned as unsuitable for personal and family life, in a report, published to-day, of the evidence of the Town and Country Planning Association before the Ministry of Health's advisory committee on housing for the under £5 a week family.

"Your neighbour's wireless and piano, his loud voice and parties up to 1 o'clock in the morning, not to speak of his quarrels, are intolerable," says the report. "So is the continual feeling of restraint involved in taking care yourself not to disturb your neighbour.

"Anyone who has experience in the management of property will acknowledge that quarrels between neighbours are many times more frequent in blocks of flats than on cottage estates."

The report regards the nursery school to which flat children go as a "terrible commentary on the bankruptcy of our present way of life," and urges that a national code of housing standards should be framed for the under £5 a week family (prewar figure).

The houses should be suitable for families of five, with outlook, privacy, and the placing of larder and kitchen carefully weighed and balanced, rows of semi-detached houses being varied by terraces of up to 10 or 12 houses.

"BROWNS" DAY

SMOOTHER WORKING IN BIRMINGHAM

Mr. and Mrs. Brown, of Birmingham, came to town to-day to get their new ration books and identity cards—and so did a lot of other people in the city whose names begin with BR, for this was the day allotted to them solely.

They all had a pleasant surprise, particularly the Browns. At no time did the two queues exceed more than 400 or 500 at one time. Strangely enough the line of waiting people including the Browns moved faster than the others.

At the head of the queues this morning sat a young girl with an automating adding machine. As each person passed by he or she was asked to call out how many cards and books were being applied for. It was all quite simple. By 10 a.m. the official recording read 2,800, and up to 11 a.m. it was 4,865. At 12.30 p.m. the figure was 7,300. Not all these people had been dealt with by this time, but they had at least got inside the Civic Centre, and once inside it was only a matter of a few minutes before they are out again.

"MORE AND BETTER BATHS"

"We are becoming swimming-minded," said Mr. H. A. Cole, Secretary of the Central Council of Recreative Physical Training, when he advocated "more and better baths" at a meeting of the Royal Life-Saving Society in Birmingham yesterday.

He called for more instruction in swimming and life-saving for schoolchildren as a means to a healthier post-war nation.

MORE ORANGES FOR MIDLANDS

A further supply of oranges has been received in the West Midlands, sufficient for a further 1lb to be drawn by every holder of a child's ration book (R.B.2)

Retailers will receive sufficient oranges for this purpose for a period of five days after receiving their supplies. Wholesalers have been authorised to release supplies to retailers to-morrow.

GUERRILLA FIGHTER

No uniform, no medals for her. But she's tough. She fights with her wits, her energy, her belief in England—in YOU. She's fighting now in the streets, knocking at your door asking you to join the battle by putting your back into saving. Give her a hand. Put every shilling you can into National Savings Certificates—either through your Savings Group, the Post Office Savings Banks, or the Birmingham Municipal Bank. Savings Certificates cost 15/-, and you can also buy them by instalments with 6d., 2/6 and 5/- Savings Stamps. *Get into the fight!*

BUY SAVINGS CERTIFICATES

"By the way, the wife's gone to Switzerland—any objection to me joining her later?"

BIRMINGHAM HOME GUARD

Signalling Certificate

This is to Certify that

(Rank) *PTE* (Name) *KENDALL*

(Batt.) *21st WARWICK H.G.*

has passed a signalling test in accordance with the require-
-ments as laid down in **Home Guard Instruction
No. 25** (Signalling) 1941, and has qualified as a
1st. Class SIGNALLER with the following results:-

BUZZER- at the rate of 6 words per minute ....*98*..%
LAMP - „ „ 4 „ „ *98*..%
FLAG - „ „ 4 „ „ *100*..%
PROCEDURE ... ...*P*.....%
WRITTEN EXAMINATION ... ...*P*....%

W.Zames

Major

Zone Communications Officer
for Colonel, Zone Commander

Birmingham Zone H.Q.   Date *22 July 43*.

B Co. 41st Warks. (B'ham) Bn. Home Guard Officers, 1943/4.

Lucas employees present a mobile canteen to the YMCA, for use with the Armed Forces, Great Hampton Street, c 1943.

"CIVVIES" FOR SOLDIERS

Relatives have to give up coupons

Many soldiers' wives, mothers, and sisters are complaining that they have to part with their personal clothes coupons to "buy" "civvies" for their men on leave.

Non-commissioned soldiers, sailors, and airmen do not have coupons of their own.

Because officers experienced the same difficulty an arrangement was made to enable them to use 21 of their personal kitting-out coupons every year to buy civilian sports clothes.

The War Office considers that "other ranks" should have sufficient civilian clothes left from pre-service days to wear during leaves. The reply from the men —particularly the younger age groups—is that they have outgrown their "civvies."

BIRMINGHAM HIPPODROME

Telephone : MIDland 2576-77

Proprietors ...	THE HAYMARKET CAPITOL LTD.
Joint Managing Directors }	{ MARK OSTRER and L. W. FARROW
Direction ...	GEORGE BLACK
Licensee and Manager ...	BERTIE ADAMS
Press Representative ...	LAWSON E. TROUT, F.Inst.P.
Musical Director ...	SYDNEY CORNESS
(THE GENERAL THEATRE CORPORATION LTD.)	

In accordance with the requirements of the Licensing Justices—
(a) The public may leave at the end of the performance by all exits and entrances other than those used as queue waiting rooms and the doors at such exits and entrances shall at the time be open. (b) All gangways, passages and staircases shall be kept entirely free from chairs or any other obstruction. (c) Persons shall not be permitted to stand or sit in any of the intersecting gangways. If standing be permitted at the rear of the seating sufficient space shall be left for persons to pass easily to and fro. (d) The fireproof curtain shall at all times be maintained in working order and shall be lowered at the beginning of and during the time of every performance.

"Alert" and "All Clear" signals will be advised to patrons by means of illuminated signs which are placed at each side of the stage. Those desiring to leave may do so, but the performance will continue.

PRICES OF ADMISSION
(Including Entertainment Tax)
Boxes 22/- and 16/6, Imperial Fauteuils 5/-, Fauteuils 4/-, Stalls 3/-, Grand Circle 4/6, Circle 3/-, Balcony 9d.

NEXT WEEK

NEWCO PRODUCTIONS
PRESENT

'SKY LARKS'
A NEW LAUGHTER SHOW
FEATURING

GEORGE DOONAN
CELIA LIPTON

AND SUPPORTING CAST

5.10   TWICE NIGHTLY   7.25
MONDAY, SEPT. 20th, 1943

LEW & LESLIE GRADE invite you to

"LAUGH AND BE HAPPY"

1 OVERTURE

2 LAUGH AND BE HAPPY with the Entire Company

3 MARIETTA DANCERS

4 ANCASTER
Unique !

5 HAL MONTY
introduces himself and introduces—

6 NAN KENWAY & DOUGLAS YOUNG
Stars of Radio's Famous Feature "Howdy Folks"
Very Tasty—Very Sweet

7 MILITARILY YOURS
Eve Clare and the Marietta Dancers

8 HAL MONTY
What a Life !

9 INTERVAL
SYDNEY CORNESS and his ORCHESTRA

10 MARIETTA DANCERS

11 "MEET MR. BROWN"
Nan Kenway & Douglas Young, Hal Monty & Eve Clare

12 BROADWAY BOYS & BRENDA
The Limit in Eccentricity

13 NAN KENWAY & DOUGLAS YOUNG

14 HAL MONTY
Laugh and Be Happy

15 MARIETTA DANCERS
introducing NAN KENWAY

16 "THE ART OF DISROBING"
as shown by EVE CLARE

17 HARRY LESTER and his HAYSEEDS
with Rufus, Gufus and Grand-pappy
Your Country Cousins come to Town

18 FINALE
The Entire Company

Manager	William Gill
Stage Manager ...	Ted Hayes
Musical Director ...	James Peverley
Production ...	Albert J. Knight
(For Lew & Leslie Grade)	

F Company, British Pens Home Guard, Bearwood Road, 1943.

LONG **S**ERVICE
CERTIFICATE

Presented to

Edward Broadbent

with the Good Wishes of the
Chairman and Directors
in appreciation of

Forty **Y**ears **S**ervice

completed on

1st December, 1943

Chairman

INSTRUCTIONS have been issued to Home Guard commanders to exclude the older men from their battle platoons.

Modern "Commando" methods of open warfare make too great a demand upon the stamina of veterans of the last war, many of them disabled by wounds, and there have recently been some cases of fatal collapse during battle exercises.

The veterans are to be posted to static jobs in their home units, I am authoritatively informed.

This should ensure that men of over 50 will not take part in exercises that are too strenuous for them.

CITY OF BIRMINGHAM.

THE DEFENCE (FIRE GUARD) REGULATIONS, 1943.
REGISTRATION FOR FIRE GUARD DUTIES.
UNDER THE FIRE GUARD (LOCAL AUTHORITY SERVICES) ORDER, 1943.

NOTICE TO REGISTER FOR MEN AGED 18—62 AND WOMEN AGED 20—44.

Any person who, after October 9, 1943, becomes registrable under the Fire Guard (Local Authority Services) Order, 1943, by reason that he or she—

(a) begins to live in the City of Birmingham to which the Order applies; or

(b) attains the age of 18 years if a male or 20 years if a female; or

(c) ceases to be a person of any of the exempted classes referred to in the 2nd Schedule to the Order;

must within 21 days after the date on which he or she becomes so registrable, report that fact in writing to the Fire Guard Office, Civic Centre, Broad Street, Birmingham 1, where forms for that purpose and information as to exemptions may be obtained.

This Direction does not apply to any person now living in the City of Birmingham and who has already registered in the said City pursuant to the said Order.

F. H. C. WILTSHIRE,
Town Clerk.

The Council House,
Birmingham 1.

PENALTIES.

Any person who fails to comply with the requirements of the Order to register or who furnishes information which he or she knows to be false in any material particular, commits an offence under the Defence (General) Regulations, 1939, involving liability to heavy penalties.

CITY OF BIRMINGHAM

EMERGENCY POWERS (DEFENCE)

FIRE GUARD.

Certificate
B/469

For the purposes of Article 11 (1) (a) and the Second Schedule, Part II (8) of the Fire Guard (Business and Government Premises) Order, 1943.

This is to certify that

Mr. Thomas Henry Yearsley

of 18 Witherford Way, Birmingham, 29,

has been appointed a Fire Guard

Street Fire Party Leader

in the area of the Local Authority and is thereby exempted from duties pursuant to the Fire Guard (Business and Government Premises) Order, 1943, except duties during his working hours under arrangements in force for any non-residential premises.

Dated this 22nd day of November 1943.

*Authorised Officer for and on behalf of
the Local Authority.*

This certificate is the property of the Local Authority, and must be surrendered on the cessation of the said duties.

P35982 B2 (a) 1339/16

CHINESE MISSION AT BOURNVILLE.

FOUR members of the Chinese Mission who have been touring this country paid a visit to Bournville on December 17th. They were received by Dame Elizabeth Cadbury, Chairman of the Bournville Village Trust, and by Mr. Paul Cadbury on behalf of the Firm. They made a short tour of the Estate and called at the Continuation School, where a Christmas party was in progress, and at the Works saw something of the Cocoa Block. After tea, Mr. Paul Cadbury spoke on the research work in housing and town planning which is being financed by the Village Trust and that which is being carried out by the West Midlands Group on Post-war Reconstruction and Planning, particularly as regards the distribution of industry. The guests asked many pertinent questions and touched also on a number of points of industrial administration. The visit was under the auspices of the Ministry of Information.

WHEN a soldier returns to this country from overseas and marries an officer or member of the ATS to whom he had been engaged, she is to be granted the same amount of leave as married ATS whose husbands have returned.

Such ATS can claim:—

Husband returned for a limited period after an absence of over one year, maximum fifty-six days (twenty-eight days paid, twenty-eight days unpaid).

Husband returned on sixty-one days' leave instead of returning on the Python scheme, twenty-eight days paid, remainder to be covered by relegation to the unemployed list.

Husband returned on thirty days' leave in lieu of Python from BLA, thirty days paid.

Husband returned on Python scheme; paid leave for the same period as his disembarkation leave.

Husband returned prisoner of war; forty-two days paid leave

Ein Volk, ein Reich, ein Führer!

"One People, one Reich, one Leader!"

WHAT will Hitler do now that grim fate is overtaking him and all his dreams of political grandeur and military glory are evaporating?

Will he fight on, or will he flee for his life?

Will he end his life in some spectacular way, as those who have known him long enough have always suspected he might if things went wrong, or will he give himself up to the Allies in a spirit of self-immolation, to die dramatically for the cause of Nazism in the belief that in his way he can best perpetuate his cruel creed?

He has always boasted about his strong nerves and urged those around him to keep cool heads. Strong nerves have always been one of his favourite themes, which is something probably not very unusual in a masochist.

Henry Street/Heneage Street, Aston, 1944.

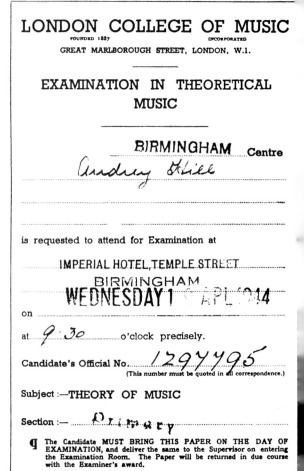

B.C.S. Ltd.
Card 40.

BIRMINGHAM
CO-OPERATIVE SOCIETY, LTD.

Registered Office : HIGH STREET, BIRMINGHAM.

Member's No. _138461_

Name _Grace Mary Lockwood_

INSTRUCTIONS.

1.—Always remember that the above is the number of your Pass Book.

2.—After making a purchase tell the shopman your number and get from him a paper Check bearing that number, and the amount of your purchase.

3.—Always put your Share number on every order for goods.

4.—Remember that if a member gives, or a shopman writes a wrong number, the dividend on that purchase will be drawn by the wrong person.

5.—Members are particularly desired to file each check and compare the amount of their purchases quarterly.

6.—Keep the checks until the voucher has been received with the amount of purchases credited, and, if incorrect, apply to office.

7.—Bring your Pass Book during the third week of quarter, and leave at the office or store.

This card is necessary to obtain admission to Quarterly or Mid-quarterly Meetings and/or for the purpose of voting at the Registered Office of the Society for the election of President, Auditor, General Committee, and Educational Committee.

RECORD OF VOTING AT HIGH STREET PREMISES.

		SEP 1943	MAR 1944

THE BIRMINGHAM PRINTERS, LIMITED, 42, HILL STREET

LONDON COLLEGE OF MUSIC
FOUNDED 1887   INCORPORATED

GREAT MARLBOROUGH STREET, LONDON, W.1.

EXAMINATION IN THEORETICAL MUSIC

BIRMINGHAM Centre

Audrey Hill

is requested to attend for Examination at

IMPERIAL HOTEL, TEMPLE STREET BIRMINGHAM

on WEDNESDAY 1ST APL 1944

at _9.30_ o'clock precisely.

Candidate's Official No. _1294495_
(This number must be quoted in all correspondence.)

Subject :—THEORY OF MUSIC

Section :— _Primary_

¶ The Candidate MUST BRING THIS PAPER ON THE DAY OF EXAMINATION, and deliver the same to the Supervisor on entering the Examination Room. The Paper will be returned in due course with the Examiner's award.

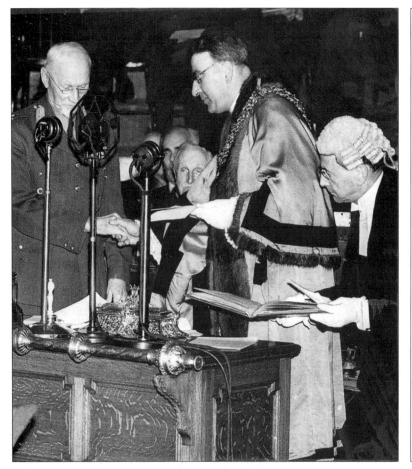

South African Premier, General Smuts, receives the Freedom of the City from the Lord Mayor, Ald. Lionel Alldridge, Town Hall, 19th May 1944.

VILLA NEWS & RECORD - - - - - - May 13th, 1944

SMART'S "SYLVANDALE" SAUSAGE
THE PERFECT WARTIME QUALITY.

TEAMS FOR SATURDAY,
— MAY 13th, 1944 —

Match No. 25.   CHARITY MATCH.   Kick off 3.0 p.m.

PORTSMOUTH

RIGHT   LEFT

WALKER

ROCHFORD (2)   SUMMERBEE (3)

GUTHRIE (4)   HARRIS (5)   DICKINSON (6)

WORRALL (7)   BUCKINGHAM (8)   DRAKE (9)   BARLOW (10)   PARKER (11)

REFEREE : Mr. B. AMES (Redditch).
LINESMEN : Mr. H. BRYAN (Tipton)
Mr. A. J. SOUTHALL (Halesowen)

HOUGHTON (11)   IVERSON (10)   PARKES (9)   EDWARDS (8)   BROOME (7)

STARLING (6)   CALLAGHAN (5)   MASSIE (4)

CUMMINGS (3)   POTTS (2)

WAKEMAN

LEFT   RIGHT

ASTON VILLA

In the event of any alteration in the teams as printed, a Board giving particulars will be sent round the ground.

SMART'S "SYLVANDALE" PIES
MAXIMUM MEAT CONTENT.   SEASONED TO PERFECTION.

WHEN you are feeling run down, go to the nearest hostal.

Spend a morning playing games the open. do a course of physical exercises. or perhaps some handicraft. Have a midday meal at the hospital and attend a lecture or "Brains Trust" in the afternoon. Rest a while and go home in the evening "rehabilitated."

That is the prospect which Mr. Willink. Minister of Health, has opened to every man, woman, and child in this country.

As part of the continuing war effort, local girls take on the unusual job (for that time) of forming a barge crew, Tyseley Wharf, 27th May 1944.

CHANCELLOR OF EXCHEQUER,
Treasury Chambers,
Great George Street,
S.W.1.

5th June, 1944.

Dear Sir,

The Chancellor of the Exchequer is very grateful to your Company for lending the further sum of £25,000 to the country free of interest, making up the amount lent in this way to £55,000.

Sir John Anderson would be glad if you would convey to the Directors his warm appreciation of the spirit which prompts this help in the War effort.

A certificate will be sent to you shortly giving title to repayment of the further loan.

Yours faithfully,

N. Tucker.

The Secretary,
Messrs. Jarrett, Rainsford & Laughton Ltd.

BSA, Small Heath, c 1944.

DEDICATION

In this hour not only the armed forces battling across the waters but the whole nation is under test. Believing that God is using us to fulfil His high purpose, the King last night broadcast, in words which lift up the heart, a call to his people to dedicate themselves anew in the crusading spirit of the dark days of 1940. This is the message which his Majesty sends:

"Four years ago our Nation and Empire stood alone against an overwhelming enemy, with our backs to the wall. Tested as never before in our history, in God's providence we survived that test; the spirit of the people, resolute, dedicated, burned like a bright flame, lit surely from those Unseen Fires which nothing can quench.

MORE NEWS ABOUT JAP CAPTIVES

The Government has published a 16-page handbook giving information about prisoners of war in the Far East. Next of kin will be given free copies soon.

This is the first step taken by the new Government Bureau which Mr. Anthony Eden told Parliament yesterday now exists to deal with inquiries from relatives of Far East prisoners.

SIRENS TEST TO-MORROW

There will be a full test of all air raid warning sirens in the West Midlands at noon to-morrow. The test will comprise: "Raiders passed" signal for one minute; short interval; "alert" signal for one minute; short interval; "raiders passed" signal for one minute.

The test will not take place if actual "alert" conditions exist at noon or have occurred between Tuesday midnight and noon.

QUIET tip to women from the National Hairdressers' Federation—Don't have a cold permanent wave till well after the war—it's dangerous.

Not because the system is bad in itself. America has taken up the idea and many of the most famous stores advertise "Cold Perms" for sale at about 10s. a packet for home use.

The trouble is, according to the National Executive of the N.H.F., that the right chemicals are being put to much more serious use just now, and are not on the market for beauty purposes.

BRIGHTER BIRMINGHAM, 1944

HERE IS THE

HOLIDAYS-AT-HOME PROGRAMME

FOR

JUNE 26TH TO JULY 8TH

ZONES 1 and 5

PRINCIPAL VENUES

HANDSWORTH PARK (Zone 1).		SUMMERFIELD PARK (Zone 5).	
Mon., June 26—Play	7.30	Mon., June 26—Parade	8. 0
Tues., „ 27—Band Contest	7.15	Tues., „ 27—Concert	7.15
Wed., „ 28—Variety	7.30	Wed., „ 28—Choir	7.30
Thurs., „ 29—Costume Dancing	2. 0	Thurs., „ 29—Physical Culture	
Thurs., „ 29—Costume Dancing	7.30	Display	7.30
Fri., „ 30—Rabbit Show	2. 0	Fri., „ 30—A.T.C. Display	7.30
Fri., „ 30—Band	7. 0	Sat., July 1—Variety	7.30
Sat., July 1—Rabbit Show	2. 0	Sun., „ 2—Band	3. 0
Sat., „ 1—Variety	7. 0	Mon., „ 3—Dancing	6. 0
Sun., „ 2—Band	3. 0	Tues., „ 4—Concert	7.30
Mon., „ 3—Service	8. 0	Wed., „ 5—Sports	6.30
Tues., „ 4—Variety	7.30	Thurs., „ 6—Sports	6.30
Wed., „ 5—Scout Rally	7.30	Fri., „ 7—Dancing	6.30
Wed., „ 5—Band	7.30	Sat., „ 8—Band	3. 0
Thurs., „ 6—Cycle Polo	7.15	Sat., „ 8—Play	7. 0
Sat., „ 8—Band	3. 0		
Sat., „ 8—Band	7. 0		

SMALL HEATH PARK (Zone 5).		TOWER STREET RECREATION GROUND	
		(St. Paul's) (Zone 1).	
Mon., June 26—A.T.C. Display	8. 0	Mon., June 26—Opening Parade	7.30
Tues., „ 27—Youth Club Display	7.30	Tues., „ 27—Variety	7. 0
Wed., „ 28—Variety	7.30	Wed., „ 28—Variety	7. 0
Thurs., „ 29—Talent Spotting	7.30	Thurs., „ 29—Band	6.30
Fri., „ 30—Boys' Brigade Night	7.30	Fri., „ 30—Variety	6.30
Sat., July 1—Exhibition Tennis	3. 0	Sat., July 1—Dance	7.30
Sat., „ 1—Dance	7.30	Sun., „ 2—Service	7.30
Sun., „ 2—Drumhead Service	3.30	Mon., „ 3—Boxing	6. 0
Mon., „ 3—Fire Guard Display	7.30	Tues., „ 4—Puppets	7. 0
Tues., „ 4—Girl Guides Night	7. 0	Wed., „ 5—Dance	7.30
Wed., „ 5—Lawn Tennis	3. 0	Thurs., „ 6—Children's Concert	7.30
Thurs., „ 6—Boy Scouts Night	7. 0	Fri., „ 7—Variety	7. 0
Fri., „ 7—Dance	7.15	Sat., „ 8—Baby Show	2.30
Sat., „ 8—Garden Fete	3. 0	Sat., „ 8—Variety	7.15

MONICA HOTEL (Small Heath) (Zone 5).		GARRISON LANE RECREATION	
		GROUND (Zone 5).	
Mon., June 26—Dance	7. 0	Mon., June 26—Band	7.15
Tues., „ 27—Variety	7. 0	Tues., „ 27—Dancing	7.15
Wed., „ 28—Dance	7.30	Wed., „ 28—Variety	7.15
Tues., July 4—Variety	7.15	Tues., July 4—Concert	7.15
Wed., „ 5—Dance	7. 0	Wed., „ 5—Variety	7.15
Fri., „ 7—Dance	7.15	Fri., „ 7—Band	7.15
		Sat., „ 8—Variety	7.15

MARQUEE (COMMON LANE, SHELDON)		MUNICIPAL SPORTS GROUND (Yardley)	
(Zone 5).		(Zone 5).	
Mon., June 26—Dance	7. 0	Mon., June 26—Dance	7. 0
Tues., „ 27—Variety	7.30	Tues., „ 27—A.T.C. Display	7.30
Wed., „ 28—A.T.C. Display	7. 0	Wed., „ 28—Ju Jitsu	7. 0
Thurs., „ 29—Whist Drive	7. 0	Tues., July 4—A.T.C. Display	7.30
Fri., „ 30—Dance	7. 0	Thurs., „ 6—Variety	7.30
Sat., July 1—Fete	3. 0	Fri., „ 30—Maypole	7.30
Mon., „ 3—Boxing	6.30	Sat., July 1—Fete	2. 0
Tues., „ 4—Variety	7. 0	Mon., „ 3—First Aid Display	7. 0
Wed., „ 5—Handicraft		Tues., „ 4—Variety	7. 0
Exhibition	7. 0	Wed., „ 5—Youth Parade	7.30
Thurs., „ 6—Whist Drive	7. 0	Fri., „ 7—Baseball	7. 0
Fri., „ 7—Variety	7. 0	Sat., „ 8—Variety	7. 0
Sat., „ 8—Sports	3. 0		

FOLLOWED BY FORTNIGHTLY FETES IN OTHER ZONES.

CUT THIS OUT FOR REFERENCE.

THE MIDLAND MUSIC CLUB

ANNOUNCE

SIX SUBSCRIPTION CONCERTS ON WEDNESDAYS AT 7 P.M.

QUEEN'S COLLEGE CHAMBERS, PARADISE STREET.

July 12th	...	ASTRA DESMOND	
Aug. 2nd	...	LEON GOOSSENS (oboe) GERALD MOORE (piano)	
Aug. 16th	...	THE GRILLER QUARTET	
Aug. 30th	...	PAULINE JULER (clarinet) MANTLE-CHILDE (piano)	
Sept. 13th	...	CYRIL SMITH PHYLLIS SELLICK } (two pianos)	
Oct. 4th	...	THE AMADIO TRIO (flute, cello, piano)	

SUBSCRIPTIONS—21/- for the series—should be sent to The Hon. Sec., Mrs. M. Field, 46, Edward Street, West Bromwich.

TOWN HALL, TUESDAY, JULY 18TH, AT 6.15 P.M.

THE

LONDON PHILHARMONIC ORCHESTRA

(Direct from their successful season at the "Proms")

CONDUCTOR - FISTOULARI.

Programme :—VERDI : Overture, "The Force of Destiny." TCHAIKOVSKY : Suite, Pique Dame. Symphony No. 2. BRAHMS : Symphony No. 1.

| Tickets: Lower Gallery | 5/6 | 6/6 | 7/6 | Upper Gallery | 6 6 |
| Ground Floor— | 3/6 | 4/6 | 5/6 | Orchestra - - | 2/6 |

BOX OFFICE NOW OPEN. NO TELEPHONE BOOKINGS.

ALL POSTAL BOOKINGS MUST BE ACCOMPANIED BY A STAMPED ADDRESSED ENVELOPE.

CONCERT DIRECTION:

W. H. PRIESTLEY & SONS, LTD., 112-113, New Street, Birmingham.

Workers from Coventry Road Garage, c 1944.

ALLIED ARMIES BEGAN THE LIBERATION OF EUROPE EARLY YESTERDAY MORNING WHEN THE GREATEST INVASION OF ALL TIME WAS LAUNCHED WITH LANDINGS FROM SEA AND AIR AT SEVERAL POINTS ON THE COAST OF NORMANDY. LATE LAST NIGHT FIGHTING WAS GOING ON IN THE STREETS OF CAEN, AN IMPORTANT ROAD JUNCTION 10 MILES INLAND AT THE BASE OF THE CHERBOURG PENINSULA.

White Hart, Bracebridge Street/Aston Road, 1944.

54

F5 Sector Staff Officers, 1944.

In the years when our Country

was in mortal danger

L/CPL DICKERS A.R.

who served May 1940 to 31st December 1944.

gave generously of his time and

powers to make himself ready

for her defence by force of arms

and with his life if need be.

George R.I.

THE HOME GUARD

Let's make it
another great
Savings year!
We've got to
keep on saving
to help win
the war...
and for the tasks
which lie ahead

Parties to   *Lest we forget*   Wounded

Under the Auspices of the   Alexandra Musical Society.

The wounded Sailors, Soldiers, Airmen,
and Merchantmen who attended the party
given by

Birmingham District Co-Operative Guild
on *Feb 23rd 1945* at *Co-Operative Cafe*

wish to convey their grateful thanks for the
kind hospitality extended to them.

The party was much enjoyed by all.

*ERNEST C. THOMAS, Hon. Organising Secretary,
Alexandra Musical Society, 249, Albert Road, Aston, Birmingham, 6.*

The girls of Jarrett, Rainsford and Laughton, Alvechurch Road,
West Heath, 1945.

CASUALTY lists in this war, 1939-1945, cannot yet be listed finally, obviously. But these are figures given by Mr. Churchill in April:

1939—1945

	Killed	Missing	Wounded	Prisoners	Totals
U. Kingdom ..	216,287	30,967	255,142	183,242	685,638
Canada	31,439	4,163	45,251	8,367	89,220
Australia	19,430	6,955	35,595	25,276	87,256
N. Zealand ..	9,334	934	17,978	8,501	36,747
S. Africa	6,030	512	12,632	14,629	33,803
Colonies	5,044	14,014	4,840	6,754	30,652
India	19,420	13,327	51,038	79,701	163,486
Totals	306,984	70,872	422,476	326,470	1,126,802

1914—1918

For the first World War, 1914 to 1918, the Empire casualties were:

	Deaths	Wounded
Gt. Britain & Ireland	812,317	1,849,494
Canada ..	62,817	166,105
Australia	60,456	154,722
N. Zealand	18,212	45,946
S. Africa..	9,032	17,843
Colonies ..	53,653	82,163
India	73,432	84,715
Totals	1,089,919	2,400,988

RAIDS.—Blitz, buzz bomb and V-bomb killed 59,793 and injured 84,749 so much that they had to be treated in hospital—a total of 144,542.

MERCHANT NAVY. — The Germans intensified the U-boat war this time, and 30,179 Merchant Navy men are known to have been killed or are missing.

ADOLF HITLER is dead. Grand Admiral Doenitz, Commander-in-Chief of the German Navy, has been appointed the new Führer. The German radio gave the news to the world at 10.25 last night in the following words: 'It is reported from the Führer's headquarters that our Führer, Adolf Hitler, has fallen this afternoon in his command post in the Reich Chancellery, fighting to his last breath against Bolshevism.

Victory flags on top of the Co-op building, High Street, 7th May 1945.

Scale of War Gratuity

Royal Navy	Army	Royal Air Force	Monthly rate gratuity
Ratings and Other Ranks			
Ordinary Seaman Able Seaman	Private Lance-Corporal	A.C.II A.C.I L.A.C.	10
Leading Seaman	Corporal Lance-Sergeant	Corporal	12
Petty Officer	Sergeant	Sergeant	14
Chief Petty Officer	Staff-Sergeant	Flight Sergeant	16
—	Warrant Officer II	—	18
—	Warrant Officer I	Warrant Officer	20
Officers			
Midshipman Acting Sub-Lieut.	Second Lieutenant	Acting Pilot Officer Pilot Officer	25
Warrant Officer Sub-Lieut.	Lieutenant	Flying Officer	30
Commissioned Warrant Officer	—	—	32
Lieutenant	Captain	Flight Lieutenant	35
Lieut.-Commander	Major	Squadron Leader	40
Commander	Lieut.-Colonel	Wing Commander	45
Captain	Colonel	Group Captain	50
Commodore 1st or 2nd Class	Brigadier	Air Commodore	55
Rear Admiral	Major General	Air Vice-Marshal	60
Vice Admiral	Lieut.-General	Air Marshal	65
Admiral	General	Air Chief Marshal	70
Admiral of the Fleet	Field Marshal	Marshal of the R.A.F.	75

Note : The above War Gratuities are not payable to certain categories of personnel who are not on Service rates of pay.

The war in the West is over. Full, unconditional surrender to the Western Allies and to Russia was made by the Germans at Gen. Eisenhower's headquarters at Rheims, at 2.41 a.m. French time to-day. Jodl, Wehrmacht Chief of Staff, signed for the Germans.

An American soldier reads the Evening Despatch and the news of VE Day, 8th May 1945

Mr. Churchill made the eagerly-awaited official announcement of the end of the war in Europe in a VE-Day broadcast to the nation this afternoon.

Hostilities will formally cease at one minute after midnight to-night, but in order to save lives the " cease fire " was actually sounded yesterday, he said.

VICTORY

VE party in Lingard Street, Nechells.

LORD MAYOR'S MESSAGE

'I AM PROUD OF BIRMINGHAM"

The Lord Mayor's Parlour,
The Council House,
Birmingham 1.

VE-DAY.

The great moment is here. The swift, significant events of recent days detract nothing from its greatness, from our profound sense of relief, nor from our proud recognition of the gallantry of every fighting man in the British Navy, Army and Air Force and in the fighting Services of our gallant Allies.

I say with all reverence and rejoicing " Thank God."

On this day of days let each one of us give thanks either at our usual or nearest place of worship, or in our own home, or at our work.

To-morrow at 11 a.m. at the Hall of Memory we hold a general Service of Thanksgiving—no one of any religious denomination or belief is excluded.

Yes, I am proud of Birmingham and its citizens. The City has known many dark and anxious days and thousands have lost their loved ones—we think of them very specially at this moment. Thousands of us still have our loved ones away, many still in danger or as prisoners of war. May God grant us true understanding of this His supreme gift—the gift of Freedom. I hope we can keep the clear knowledge of it throughout our lives and, to our little utmost, help build that better world which can be made given less selfishness on all our parts.

We will do well to heed the recent words of our Prime Minister and rejoice soberly, conscious of the great task still ahead. The citizens of a city which, in its workshops, offices and services, has played so great a part in the achievement of this long-sought Victory, need no call from me to celebrate that Victory thankfully, cheerfully and worthily.

W. T. WIGGINS-DAVIES,
Lord Mayor.

VE Day celebrations by Galloways Corner, New Street, 8th May 1945.

VE Day, New Street.

During the Victory Parade, the Lord Mayor, W.T. Wiggins-Davis meets members of the McGeoch Works Fire Brigade, 13th May 1945.

~~~The Price of Victory~~~

TOTAL casualties suffered during the war by the Armed Forces, Auxiliary Services and the civilian population of the U.K. were 950,794. Of these 357,116 were killed ; 369,267 wounded ; 78,332 prisoners of war or internees ; 46,079 missing. Those killed in the Services were— Royal Navy, 50,758 ; Army, 144,079 ; R.A.F., 39,606. Navy wounded, 14,663 ; Army 239,575 ; R.A.F., 22,839. Civilians killed, 60,595 ; wounded, 86,182 ; Merchant Navy and Fishing Fleets, killed, 30,248 ; wounded, 4,707 ; Women's Services, killed, 624 ; wounded, 744 ; Home Guard, killed, 1,206 ; wounded, 557.

No big rush for basic petrol in Birmingham on first day of issue

IT is easy to get your basic ration coupons for petrol providing your car is already licensed. There was a brisk demand in Birmingham for basic ration petrol coupons, the issue of which began to-day, for vehicles already licensed, though there was nothing in the nature of a rush during the morning.

The British cruiser, HMS Birmingham, berthed in Copenhagen, May 1945.

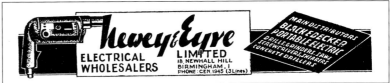

P. 34 W. 34, goals for 269, against 26

I have received details of the outstanding football record of a Birmingham A.T.C. Squadron, 477 B.S.A.

During the season they played 34 matches and they won the lot, scoring 269 goals against 26.

Then the matches were not confined to Birmingham, for in winning the Sir Albert Ball Cup they came up against teams in the Midland Command. Their six matches in that competition yielded them 35 goals against six.

In winning the A.F.C. Cup (Birmingham Wing) they scored 44 goals against six in five matches, and the A.T.C. League Cup (South Division) yielded 63 goals against one in five matches.

James, the squadron's leading marksman, scored 91 goals in 22 appearances—an average of over four goals per match.

The pilot of an R.A.F. plane, of which he was believed to be the only occupant, was killed instantly when his machine crashed into a gorse-covered slope on the Lickey Hills, near Barnt Green, shortly after 9 o'clock this morning.

Identification of the pilot of the plane is difficult, as the machine burst into flames and was completely destroyed.

A youth working in the rickyard of the Yew Tree Farm, Lower Shepley, saw the plane dive low, apparently out of control and with smoke pouring from the engine. It buried itself in the ground and there were two loud explosions.

The youth ran to the spot and found the body of the pilot lying near a brook, with his parachute nearby.

Bromsgrove N.F.S. and police were called, and R.A.F. personnel took charge of the wreckage.

NEW GOVERNMENT CHOSEN

STATE of the Parties after the polling on July 1945, and subsequently, was as follows: Tw results remained to be announced. Labour registere a large majority over all other parties.

Conservative	—	—	—	—	200
National	—	—	—	—	2
Liberal National	—	—	—	—	13
Liberal	—	—	—	—	1

The foregoing represented the Nation's vote fc the Government : total, 216.

Labour	—	—	—	—	393
Liberal	—	—	—	—	11
I.L.P.	—	—	—	—	3
Communist	—	—	—	—	2
Irish Nationalist	—	—	—	—	2
Common Wealth	—	—	—	—	1
Independent	—	—	—	—	8

Total for the Opposition, 420.

Gains and losses, as declared on July 26, were Labour, 215 gains, 4 losses ; Conservative, 7 gains 183 losses ; Liberals, 3 gains, 11 losses Thirty-twe members of the Caretaker Government lost thei seats. Of the Labour M.P.s 119 were trade unionists half of them under 40, and 126 had come straigh from the Services. Total of votes (which, all told represented more than 75 per cent of the electorate registered for Mr. Churchill's Government (July 26 was 10,075,283 ; against, 14,874,951.

The new May Queen, Pauline Timerick, is crowned by her predecessor, Betty Hoyse, Tinkers Farm Secondary School, Northfield, 11th May 1945.

Victor Yates, Labour MP for Ladywood, talks to Mrs Mary Hughes during his celebratory tour after winning the constituency, 1945.

VJ Day in Miller Street, Aston,
15th August 1945.

```
                THE WARREN HILL RD.VICTORY FUND
                        BALANCE SHEET

       INCOME                           EXPENDITURE
                    £.  s.  d.                    £.  s.  d    £.  s.  d
Cash C/F from VE Day    16.  7   CATERING
Weekly Contributions 36. 19.  6   Mrs Enticknap    14.  1.  4½
Collection Aug.15th  15. 19.  0   B'ham Dairy Co.  15.  0. 10
 "   School Aug.16th  2.  8.  6   Cordials          3. 13.  6
Donations             4. 16. 10   Ice Cream         1.  9.  0
From Resale of Food   1.  7.  1½                               34.  4.  8½
 "     "     " Cordials 1.  1.  6  SPORTS                        5.  0.  0
                                  Fancy Dress,Spot Prizes etc. 4. 0. 0
                    £63.  9.  0½    "       "   Childrens        14.  0
                                  Souvenirs                     9. 15.  0
                                  Hall Hire        1. 10. 10
                                   "   Caretaker   1. 15.  0
Signed  ..D.C.Jones.. Auditor                                  3.  5. 10
                                  Lighting                         7.  6
        ..D.Page..... Auditor     Records 3 ea 4.2d             12.  6
                                  Stationary                     3. 10
        ..A.Badsey... Secretary   Balance. Cash in Hand        5.  5.  8

                                                    £63.  9.  0½
```

Pupils at Glengarry Private School, High Street,
Harborne, 1945. The teacher is the Principal,
Miss Ethel Marshall.

WITH war production ending, British car manufacturers hope to double their target of 200,000 cars for this year.

Export trade will be the main consideration.

"Accumulated world demand must amount to at least £500,000,000," Mr. H. D. Simmons, of the Society of Motor Manufacturers and Traders, said yesterday.

"It is up to Britain to supply the cars.

"Our present target is only half normal peace output. We shall need to more than double it if all demands are to be met.

"Factories will be able to switch to civilian production very quickly. If demobilisation is speeded up there will be no shortage of labour.

"Providing there is no delay in releasing materials there is no need for unemployment in the motor industry."

Austin 10's being loaded onto an Avro-York, for exportation to South Africa, September 1945.

The King and Queen, accompanied by Princess Margaret, step ashore from HMS Birmingham, after an inspection of the Home Fleet, the Firth of Forth, 28th September 1945.

Will Fyffe, Scotland's great comedian, headlines the bill at the Hippodrome, 29th October 1945.

Birmingham City Police.

This is to certify that _John Edward Jones_ joined the Birmingham Police, as Constable, on the _Sixteenth_ day of _October_ One thousand nine hundred and _Eleven_ and left his Situation in the rank of _Sergeant_ on the _Thirtieth_ day of _December_ One thousand nine hundred and _Forty-five_ having _been pensioned on completion of service_

Character.

"His conduct was exemplary"

Description of _J. E. Jones_ ¶

Age   52 Years.
Height   6 Feet 2 Inches.
Complexion.   Fresh.
Eyes   Hazel.
Hair   Fair.
Particular Marks   Scar. L. forehead.
Figure   Proportionate.

Given under my hand, and seal of the Birmingham Police.

CHIEF CONSTABLE.

Newton Street, Birmingham.

_30th_ day of _December_ 19_45_.

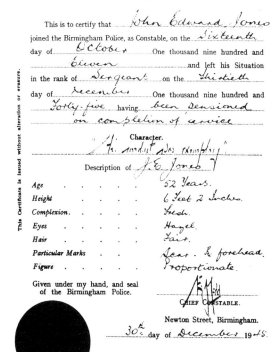

LUNCHEON

AT THE COUNCIL HOUSE

IN HONOUR OF THE
VISIT OF THEIR MAJESTIES
THE KING AND QUEEN

ALDERMAN W. T. WIGGINS-DAVIES J.P. LORD MAYOR

NOVEMBER 7TH 1945

The King and Queen arrive at the Accident Hospital, 7th November 1945.

1946

PRIME MINISTER'S APPEAL TO THE NATION'S WORKERS

TEAM SPIRIT TO WIN WAR AGAINST WANT

Broadcasting an appeal to the nation to work for more production, the Prime Minister on Sunday said: "I have not the slightest doubt that we shall come triumphantly through this testing time of 1946 just as we came through 1940." He said that work was the only way to get the goods so badly needed, and urged all classes to "march forward together cheerfully, to win the war against want."

Warmington Road residents' party,
Stanville Road Junior and Infants' School, Sheldon, 1946.

Handsworth Girls' Training Corps., 1946.

The bomb-damaged Metropole Cinema may re-open for stage shows, Snow Hill, 16th March 1946.

THE British farmer was called on in the Commons yesterday to make still greater efforts to produce food, and was offered some financial encouragement by the Government to do so.

Mr. T. Williams (Minister of Agriculture) told the House that in view of the world food crisis it was essential to plough up some land which had been laid down to seed when it was thought that more livestock and less cereals could safely be produced.

17599   Army Form X 202/B.

CERTIFICATE OF TRANSFER to the ARMY RESERVE

Army No. 5254902   Rank *Corporal*

Surname (Block letters) BROADBENT.

Christian Name(s) *Stanley.*

Regt. or Corps *The Worcestershire Regiment*

The transfer of the above-named to the appropriate Class of the Army Reserve (see note below) is confirmed with effect from *14.4.46* .

*The date to be inserted here will be that following the day on which Release Leave terminates, including any additional leave to which the soldier may be entitled by virtue of service overseas.

Note.—The appropriate Class of the Army Reserve is as follows :—

Rowheath Pavilion and Lido, 1946.

During a tour of factories, showing the different manufacturing industries housed in the city, organised by the Chamber of Commerce, the Lord Mayor, Ald. Alan Giles, chats to Mr. W. Macleod, Messrs. George Ellison Ltd. (switch gear manufacturers), Wellhead Lane, Perry Barr, 9th May 1946.

The newly-renovated drinking fountain in Temple Row, 1946.

TUESDAY WILL BE REMNANT DAY at LEWIS'S

Hundreds of useful lengths of Wools, Rayons, Spuns and Cotton Fabrics. Sold by weight! Four coupons for 1 lb. approximate weight. Come early next Tuesday.

The BOY and GIRL STORY

LEWIS'S have been specialists in Children's Clothing for nearly 100 years, and this knowledge, plus the backing of Lewis's straightforward policy of satisfaction guaranteed or money refunded, is the reason why so many mothers buy their children's clothing at Lewis's. You can rely on Lewis's.

---- CUT THIS OUT AND KEEP IT AS A GUIDE ·----

How to get your new Ration Book

WHERE TO GO IN BIRMINGHAM
WHEN: 10th JUNE to 6th JULY, 1946

HOURS: Mondays to Fridays: 9 a.m. to 6.30 p.m.
Saturdays: 9 a.m. to 4. 0 p.m.

WEEK 3: 10th JUNE to 15th JUNE, 1946					
Mon.	Tues.	Wed.	Thurs.	Fri	Sat.
CLOSED	Ga-Go	Gr-Gz	Ha-Hi	Ho	Hu-Hz

Cen. No.	DISTRICT	DISTRIBUTION CENTRE
1	CITY	Civic Centre
2	ASTON	Victoria Road Baths
3	BALSALL HEATH	Moseley Road Baths
4	ERDINGTON	Mason Road, Erdington
5	HANDSWORTH	Grove Lane Baths
6	HARBORNE	Harborne Baths
7	KING'S HEATH	King's Heath Baths, Institute Road
8	KINGSTANDING	Kingstanding Baths, Warren Farm Rd.
9	LADYWOOD	Monument Road Baths
10	NORTHFIELD	Northfield Baths, Bristol Rd. South
11	SALTLEY	George Arthur Road Baths
12	SMALL HEATH	Green Lane Baths
13	SPARKHILL	Sparkhill Baths, Stratford Road
14	YARDLEY	Church Road Schools

Any person who attend a Distribution Centre may collect Ration Books for others outside the alphabetical range allotted for the day.
Every effort should be made to call on the day allotted to the particular letter to avoid queues and congestion.
Factories, Firms, and large organisations may, as in previous years, participate in the "Block Scheme" by arranging in writing direct with the Food Executive Officer. All envelopes should be marked at the top left-hand corner "Block Scheme."

VICTORY CELEBRATION
BIRMINGHAM DISCUSSIONS

Discussion is taking place among the chairmen of the main committees of Birmingham City Council and the principal officers of the Corporation as to the best means of celebrating victory on Whit-Saturday, June 8.

They met on Monday, under the chairmanship of the Lord Mayor, and discussed the general question on the basis of a circular from the Home Office, which outlined what is to be done in London—a victory parade of the Services, entertainments in public parks concerts for the blind in public institutions, firework displays, and the illumination of public buildings.

A BRIGHTER CITY
NEED FOR PROVISION OF MORE AMUSEMENTS
ACCOMMODATION PROBLEM AT HOTELS

Some time may elapse before Birmingham people cease to go early to bed for lack of amusement, and some time before the city's hotels and restaurants can join in providing late night entertainment; but brighter Birmingham is on the way, and it has the blessing of the municipal authorities.

So much is clear from the conference on Birmingham's hotel problem, which was held under the chairmanship of the Lord Mayor of Birmingham at the Council House on Friday.

It was attended by representatives of the hotel business, railway and road transport, the Chamber of Commerce, and the licensing justices.

The most pressing need is the provision of more hotel accommodation for business men visiting the city. The conference, while going into this question, reviewed the whole problem of Birmingham's entertainment facilities and in large measure agreed that a considerable brightening of the city's " night life " is needed

SUNDAY, 9 JUNE, 1946.

LET US BE OF GOOD CHEER!

THE morning after the day before finds us perhaps wondering what it was all about. What we celebrated yesterday, with various degrees of enthusiasm, was not so much Victory as the defeat of a menace to freedom. There is not much for us to be cheerful about these days, but yesterday's occasion did at least provide a break in the monotonous gloom. We in these islands are badly in need of relief from sameness, and if we can work up a little brightness for ourselves, as most of us did yesterday, so much the better. We ought to get together more often in these victorious days of austerity and try to get a communal laugh out of our sorry mess.

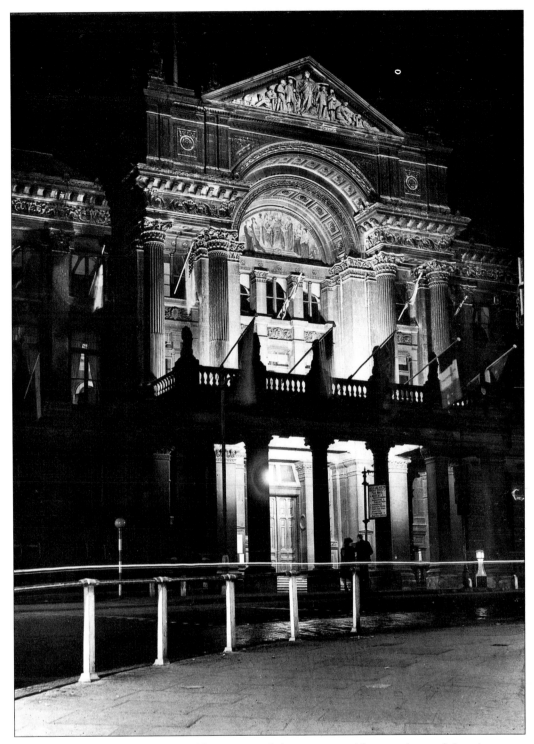

The Council House is floodlit as part of the countrywide ongoing celebrations, 8th June 1946.

Warwickshire C.C.C., Summer 1946.

LAST-MINUTE rushes for the London trains, followed by an unexpected lull, show that while Birmingham found the celebrations in the capital a big attraction, the city's main favour is a holiday at home.

Rail and bus officials were surprised yesterday to find so few people travelling.

"Considerably less than the usual holiday Saturday and less, even, than a normal Saturday," was a Midland Red official's report on the company's traffic.

On the railways, after one train had left Snow Hill for Paddington in three parts with the third carrying 750 people, yesterday brought a lull described by one traffic controller as amazing.

"Long distance travel, which we expected to draw the crowds, was very little differnt from a normal summer Saturday," he said.

Seats were available in most trains as they left Birmingham, although one to Llandudno and another to Bristol and the West were crowded.

Little demand

There was little demand for transport to the nearer holiday centres, but in anticipation of bigger crowds to-day and to-morrow additional trains have been arranged for such destinations as Evesham, Stratford, Sutton, Malvern, and Ludlow.

Racing at Wolverhampton to-morrow—the first time for six years—is also expected to produce a big exodus from Birmingham.

Birmingham Transport Department had extra crews standing by ready to run relief buses, but traffic was very light

BEGINNING ON JULY 21, 1946, rationing of bread, flour, and flour confectionery in Britain was announced by the Minister of Food in the House of Commons on June 27. Mr. Strachey stated that the Government had reached this decision because they were convinced that to fail to ration bread and flour would be to take an unjustifiable risk with the basic foodstuff of the British people. In the subsequent Parliamentary debates, Mr. Strachey disclosed that there was no great reserve store of wheat lying idle in the country ; there was only the stock going through the " pipe-line " from ships to shops. It was estimated that at the end of August there would be some eight weeks' supply of bread and flour in hand—sufficient to satisfy with certainty the bread supply of the country if a system of rationing were introduced, but not without it. Rationing enabled the authorities to work with a considerably smaller amount in the pipe-line. The basic adult ration is 9 oz. a day, with graduated amounts for children and extra allowances for manual workers

The Austin Motor Co., Longbridge, 1946.

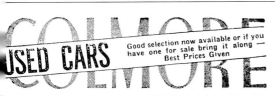
✶

CAN Birmingham produce a girl vocalist with a voice to suit Roy Fox?

ROY, who has just come to England from New York, has not found the young lady yet.

OVER 100 girls think they have a chance to make a name for themselves, and are ready to prove it.

ON their voices and good looks depend their chances at the Grand Casino, Birmingham, auditions tomorrow.

NORTH of England towns have had their chance, but no new microphone personality has been found.

EIGHT years have passed since Roy Fox's famous " whispering " trumpet was heard in this country.

RADIO listeners will therefore, in the near future, probably be hearing a Birmingham girl on the air with him.

SO sing up, girls!

Bandleader, Roy Fox, attends the auditions at the Grand Casino, 3rd July 1946.

Open air dancing in Muntz Park, Umberslade Road, Selly Park, 25th July 1946.

NEW FACTS AND FIGURES

THOUSANDS of animals and birds who played their part in the War were represented in London's Victory March, on June 8, 1946, by the Alsatians Jet and Irma. (See illus. in page 168.) These two Civil Defence Rescue Dogs, who wear the Dickin Medal—the Animals V.C.—for rescue work in air raids, are members of the Allied Forces Mascot Club of the People's Dispensary for Sick Animals. This club was formed to obtain lasting recognition for all the animals who, besides actual war work, contributed so much in maintaining morale and giving companionship to men and women of the Allied Forces.

THE Allied Forces Mascot Club, as well as compiling records for the Imperial War Museum of the wartime work of transport animals, guard and rescue dogs and homing pigeons, wishes to commemorate in a practical manner those who lost their lives. An Animals' War Memorial is to take the form of Caravan Dispensaries to bring relief to sick and suffering animals. Used throughout the War as rescue vehicles for thousands of animal raid victims, many such caravans were damaged or worn out, and the P.D.S.A. hopes to replace them by means of the Memorial funds which are now being raised by public subscription.

OF the 996 commissioned U-boats (German, Italian and Japanese) destroyed by the Allies throughout all the oceans of the world (said Mr. A. V. Alexander on March 7, 1946) over 300, or nearly one-third, were within 500 miles of the U.K.—this showing the intensity of the U-boats' concentration against the British Isles.

THE two outstanding months of the war against the U-boat were May 1943, when 46 U-boats were sunk, and April 1945, when the Germans were evacuating the Baltic ports and 65 U-boats were sent down. The month of May proved the turning-point of the war at sea: losses of Allied and neutral shipping, which averaged well over 20,000 tons daily in 1942 and over 14,000 tons daily in March-May 1943, fell by June-August to under 7,000 tons, and subsequently even lower.

IN the whole course of the war (it was stated on March 7, 1946) nearly 51,000 officers and men of the Royal Navy, including the Navies of the Dominions, and of the Royal Marines, were killed or were still missing. This number exceeded by over 20,000 the numbers killed between 1914-1918. Up to the end of 1945 nearly 15,000 awards had been made to officers and men of the Royal Navy, including the Dominion Navies, Royal Marines and Reserves; these included 23 V.C.s and 29 G.C.s.

FROM the beginning of the war to August 31, 1945, H.M. ships and craft lost amounted to 3,282. The figure included three battleships and two battle cruisers, or one-third of our capital ship strength at the outbreak of the war; five fleet carriers; 23 cruisers; 134 destroyers; 77 submarines.

PEACE stamps, to commemorate the Victory celebrations, were on sale at British post-offices on June 11, 1946, when it was expected that the special issue of 264,000,000 would be exhausted in about two months. The total cash value of £2,800,000 is made up of 240,000,000 of the 2½d. denomination and 24,000,000 of the 3d. They are not available in book form, their size being double that of the ordinary stamp. The 2½d. one is blue, its design emphasizing peace through victory and reconstruction at home. The 3d. stamp, deep violet, symbolizes peace abroad. His Majesty the King made the final selection of the designs. See illus. below.

University of Birmingham, Edgbaston, c 1946.

Members of the Sparta team due to play Birmingham City at St. Andrew's on Monday are (left to right) standing: Blaha, Ludl, Koubek, Riha, Ceip, Kokstein, Zastera; kneeling: Zmatlik, Senecky, Horak, Vejvoda.

The family gathering to celebrate the Golden Wedding of Mr and Mrs Edward Cadbury, Bournville, 22nd October 1946.

The Rt. Hon. Aneurin Bevan, Minister of Health, addresses the audience at the prize-giving evening at the Queen Elizabeth Hospital, Edgbaston, 1st November 1946.

A group of semi-final winners in the Carrol Levis talent competition, Midland Institute, 5th January 1947.

Trevor Ford, transferred from Swansea Town to Aston Villa at a fee of £10,000, January 1947.

Mobile Police Station, Duke Street, Gosta Green, 20th January 1947.

Freddie Mills.

Chamberlain Square, from Ratcliff Place, March 1947.

The Bull Ring, looking towards Digbeth, March 1947.

NOW most of Birmingham's snow has disappeared and the floods are on the wane, public works officials are facing a new problem—DIRT.

A formidable clearing-up job awaits the city's workmen, who for nearly two months have been unable to attempt "spring cleaning" of the streets.

An official said to-day that it will be a considerable time before things are normal again.

Reports from Birmingham railway officials, transport managers and public works authorities show, however, that public services are steadily improving.

Flood waters in Walsall-road area at Perry Barr, are receding rapidly, though some roads are still closed to traffic.

Water in Church-road has subsided, and it is open to outward-bound traffic, but diversions are still necessary for inward-bound traffic.

Hamstead Hill is still under water and closed for transport.

Both the L.M.S. and G.W.R. state that all local services are running normally and flooding is causing little inconvenience.

Yesterday the L.M.S. moved 11,000 tons of coal from Cannock Chase collieries.

The traffic turns from Hill Street into New Street with great difficulty, 5th March 1947.

THEATRES AND CINEMAS

CINEMATOGRAPH EXHIBITORS' ASSOCIATION

THEATRE ROYAL NEW STREET, B'HAM. nees Daily (Tues. & Fri. excepted) 2.0 p.m. Evenings at 7.0 p.m. M ARNOLD & EMILE LITTLER present **OODY TWO HOES** FRED EMNEY HAYDEN HENRY LYTTON K STANFORD SMEDDLE BROS CAST OF 80 ARTISTES. Office Open 10 a.m. until 8.30 p.m.

LEXANDRA THEATRE TS. 2 (Fri. exc.), EVNGS. 7 p.m. SIMPLE SIMON 31: KEEP IT DARK, a new re. Prior to London Production. 7: POLISH PARADE. A Medley Music, Ballet and Song. 14: "WE PROUDLY PRESENT," new Play by Ivor Novello. 21: BALLETS JOOSS. 28 (to be announced). Office Open for above open 20/3/47. 5: Opening of Repertory Season.

EPERTORY THEATRE. Evenings (ex. Mon.) 6.30. Matinees inesday, Thursday, Saturday, 2.30. Sir Barry Jackson presents "HE SILENT WOMAN," By Ben Jonson. Office 10.30—7. No phone bookings. sday, April 1st: "AN IDEAL USBAND," by Oscar Wilde.

IPPODROME HURST STREET, B'HAM. 6.0. TWICE NIGHTLY. 8.15. ARTHUR ASKEY EDDIE GRAY CTOR BARNA & ALEC BROOK. THE CYCLING D'ORMONDES OR KIDDIE. JANET BROWN. MARY PRIESTMAN CYNTHIA & GLADYS. THE JAVA BROTHERS. Office Open 10.0 a.m. until 9.0 p.m.

STON HIPPODROME 6.20. TWICE NIGHTLY — 8.30 Man Who Invented Shakespeare. LEON CORTEZ of B.B.C. "HARMONY HALL," ith SPECIAL APPEARANCE of ARTHUR WHITE In "VARIETY FAIR."

DUDLEY AMUSEMENTS

DUDLEY HIPPODROME htly at 7.30. Mat. Sat. at 4.15 p.m st Performance Saturday, Mar. 22nd. S. H. NEWSOME presents ACK & THE BEANSTALK. ACK EDGE. :: ROY ROYSTON. n., March 24th—Nightly at 7.30. ats. Wed. and Thurs., 2.15 p.m.— "THE STUDENT PRINCE." Office Open 10.0 a.m. until 9.0 p.m.

COVENTRY AMUSEMENTS

IPPODROME, COVENTRY. (Phone 3141). This Week and xt Week. Evenings 6.45. Matinees Thursday and Saturday, 2.30. HE ROYAL CARL ROSA OPERA, under direction of H. B. Phillips. epertoire details apply Box Office. n., March 23rd, 7.0 p.m.: New Midland Philharmonic Orchestra. Con- 'uctor, Mathew Stevenson; Phyllis sellick and Cyril Smith. ar. 21: Evgs. 6.45. Mats. Thurs., Sat., 1.30: 'LADY WINDERMERE'S FAN.'

VEDNESBURY AMUSEMENTS

VEDNESBURY HIPPODROME / (Phone WED. 0634). Nightly at 7.15 p.m. Saturday 6 and 8.15 p.m. HE MAGNET REPERTORY CO. in MA'S BIT O' BRASS, A Comedy by Ronald Gow. FREE CAR PARK.

AMUSEMENTS

CE SKATING RINK, SUMMER HILL ROAD. CEN. 6036. At 11.0, 2.30 and 7.30. BOOTS AND SKATES NOW AVAILABLE FOR HIRE.

ODEON THEATRE, Warley. SUNDAY, MARCH 23rd. NAT LLEN WITH HIS RADIO AND ELEVISION ORCHESTRA, with ANETTE REES & JUDY DEAN. ors Open 6.30. Com. 7 p.m. Book Now.

ODEON NEW-STREET. Doors Open 10.0 a.m. Continuous until 10.30 p.m. **TEMPTATION** (A) with MERLE OBERON, GEORGE BRENT, CHARLES KORVIN, PAUL LUKAS. Screen: at 11.35, 2.46, 5.57, 8.58. Also **MR. BIG** (U) DONALD O'CONNOR, GLORIA JEAN, PEGGY RYAN, ROBERT PAIGE. Screened at 10.25, 1.24, 4.35, 7.46.

GAUMONT STEELHOUSE LANE Continuous from 12.30 p.m. DANNY KAYE VIRGINIA MAYO VERA-ELLEN in **THE KID FROM BROOKLYN** (u) With the Gorgeous Goldwyn Girls (In Technicolor) At 1.50, 5.10 and 8.25. **CANDY'S CALENDAR** (U) At 12.50, 4.10, and 7.25 MARCH OF TIME No. 1 — New Series (u)

FORUM Cont. 12.35. MID. 4549. An A.B.C. Theatre. SECOND BIG WEEK OF CARY GRANT ALEXIS SMITH in Cole Porter's **NIGHT AND DAY** (U) in Glorious Technicolor. with MONTY WOOLLEY GINNY SIMMS MARY MARTIN JANE WYMAN Screened at 12.55, 3.20, 5.50, 8.15. To-morrow Continuous from 12.35 p.m.

WEST END. MID. 0022. DOORS OPEN 11.45. COMM. 12.0 noon. GRAND ALL-BRITISH PROGRAMME JOHN MILLS. VALERIE HOBSON, BERNARD MILES in **GREAT EXPECTATIONS** (A) introducing ANTHONY WAGER. JEAN SIMMONS. Showing at 12.0, 2.50, 5.40, 8.30. FULL SUPPORTING PROGRAMME At Your Service—The West End Cafe.

FUTURIST THEATRE To-day RAY MILLAND, TERESA WRIGHT in **MRS. LORING'S SECRET** (A) 2.0, 5.10, 8.15 also FREDDIE STEWART, JUNE PREISSER in **FREDDIE STEPS OUT** (A) 12.50, 3.55, 7.0

SCALA TO DAY CONSTANCE MOORE WILLIAM MARSHALL in **HATS OFF TO RHYTHM** (U) 12.30, 3.10, 5.50, 8.25 also DONALD BARRY, ANN SAVAGE in **THE LAST CROOKED MILE** (A) 2.5, 4.45, 7.25

TATLER THEATRE STATION STREET CONTINUOUS from 10.15 A.M. PRICES 10d. AND 1/6. **DUTCH VISTA**

ADELPHI, Hay Mills (A.B.C.). VIC. 1208. John Loder, Lenore Aubert, **THE WIFE OF MONTE CRISTO** (A). Also **JOE PALOOKA, CHAMP** (A).

ALBION, New Inns, HANDSWORTH.— **SEND FOR PAUL TEMPLE** (A). Anthony Hulme, Joy Shelton; **HOW DO YOU DO-O-O?** (U), Bert Gordon.

ALHAMBRA, Moseley-rd (A.B.C.). VIC. 2826. Anna Lee, James Ellison in **G.I. WAR BRIDES** (A); and Albert Dekker, **THE FRENCH KEY** (A). News.

APOLLO — TYBURN ROAD. Randolph Scott in **BAD MAN'S TERRITORY** (A), Etc. Thursday: Magic Bow (u).

ASTORIA (A.B.C.). AST. 2384. Claudette Colbert, **WITHOUT RESERVATIONS** (A); supported by Philip Reed in **BIG TOWN** (A). News.

ATLAS, STECHFORD. — STE. 2206. **THE CHINESE BUNGALOW** (A). Kay Walsh, Paul Lukas; **THE MAN WHO LOST HIMSELF** (U), K. Francis.

BEACON — GREAT BARR. Edward G. Robinson, **THE SEA WOLF** (A). 2.20, 5.30, 8.40; **The Shadow Returns** (a). Thurs: Miss Susie Slagles

BEACON, Smethwick (A.B.C.). SME. 1045. **EPIC OF ARNHEM, THEIRS IS THE GLORY** (A). Full Supporting Programme.

BEAUFORT, WASHWOOD HEATH.— David Niven, Roger Livesey, Raymond Massey, **A MATTER OF LIFE AND DEATH** (A). Sun: This is the Life (a)

BIRCHFIELD, Perry Barr. BIR. 4333. Pat O'Brien and Ruth Warwick in **Perilous Holiday** (a); **Faithful in My Fashion** (A). Thurs: Michael Strogoff.

BRISTOL, Bristol-road (A.B.C.). CAL. 1904. Robert Donat, Emlyn Williams, **THE CITADEL** (A); Kent Taylor, **Deadline for Murder** (a).

BROADWAY, Briston-street. MID. 1761. ANNA LEE, JAMES ELLISON in **G.I. WAR BRIDES** (A), and **FRENCH KEY** (A).

CAPITOL, WARD END.—Rex Harrison, Diana Churchill in **SCHOOL FOR HUSBANDS** (A); Laurel and Hardy in **FLYING DEUCES** (A)

CARLTON, SPARKBROOK. SOU. 0861. STEWART GRANGER, PHYLLIS CALVERT in **THE MAGIC BOW** (U). Full supporting programme.

CASTLE BROMWICH CINEMA.— Karen Morley, Jim Bannon, Jeff Donnell in **THE UNKNOWN** (A); also **Blondie Knows Best** (U).

CLIFTON — GREAT BARR. **A MATTER OF LIFE AND DEATH** (A) (Tech.) 5.40, 8.20. Full Support. Sun.: Higher and Higher (A).

CORONET, SMALL HEATH. VIC. 0420. Olivia De Havilland, Lew Ayres, **THE DARK MIRROR** (A); **THE BAXTER MILLIONS** (U), Fay Holden.

CROWN, Ladywood (A.B.C.). EDG. 1122. Paul Kelly, Douglas Fowley, **GLASS ALIBI** (A); Philip Reed and Hilary Brook, **BIG TOWN** (A). News.

DANILO, LONGBRIDGE. PRI. 2470. Betty Hutton in **CROSS MY HEART** (A) at 2.15, 5.35, 9.0; Will Fyffe in **Rulers of the Sea** (U) at 3.45, 7.10.

DANILO, QUINTON. WOO 2562.— Michael Wilding in **CARNIVAL** (A), with Sally Gray; also **CLUB HAVANA** (A).

EDGBASTON, Monument-road (A.B.C.). EDG. 3273. Van Johnson & Keenan Wynn, **NO LEAVE NO LOVE** (A); also **CHILDREN ON TRIAL** (A).

ELITE — HANDSWORTH NOR. 0665. For Six Days. Birmingham's Own Hazel Court, Michael Wilding in **CARNIVAL** (A).

EMPIRE, SMETHWICK. SME. 0757. John Loder, Lenore Aubert in **THE WIFE OF MONTE CRISTO** (A); also Tom Neal in **CLUB HAVANA** (A).

GAIETY, COLESHILL ST. (A.B.C.). CEN. 6649. **WEEK-END IN HAVANA** (U), in Colour) also **RENDEZVOUS 24** (A).

EMPRESS, Sutton (A.B.C.). SUT. 2363. Robert Donat, Emlyn Williams in **THE CITADEL** (A). And Full Supporting Programme.

ERA CINEMA, BORDESLEY GREEN. Robert Young, Helen Gilbert, Lee Bowman, and Charles Coburn in **FLORIAN** (U).

GLOBE, ASTON. — AST. 0652. John Wayne in **DAKOTA** (U). **HANDS ACROSS THE OCEAN** (U).

GRAND, Soho-road, HANDSWORTH.— **FLIGHT FROM FOLLY** (A), Pat Kirkwood, Sydney Howard; also **ELMER'S OTHER TALE** (A).

GRAND, Alum Rock-road, SALTLEY. **THE LAST OUTPOST** (A), Cary Grant; **DOUBLE EXPOSURE** (A) (Chester Morris).

GRANGE, SMALL HEATH. VIC. 0434. Rex Harrison, Diana Churchill in **SCHOOL FOR HUSBANDS** (A); Laurel and Hardy in **FLYING DEUCES** (U).

GROVE CINEMA, Dudley-road. SME. 0343. **The Dark Mirror** (a), Mon. to Fri. 3.17, 6.4, 8.51; **The Baxter Millions** (u) Sun: Woman of the Town (a).

IMPERIAL, Moseley-rd. (A.B.C.). CAL. 2283. Rex Harrison, **ANNA AND THE KING OF SIAM** (A), with Irene Dunne; also **GLAMOUR GIRL** (A).

KING'S NORTON— June Haver, **THREE LITTLE GIRLS IN BLUE** (U); Philip Reed, **BIG TOWN** (A).

KINGSTON, SMALL HEATH. VIC. 2639. George Raft and Sylvia Sidney, **MR. ACE** (A); also William Boyd, in **LUMBERJACK** (A).

KINGSWAY — HIG. 1352. June Haver, George Montgomery, in **THREE LITTLE GIRLS IN BLUE** (Tech.). Screened at 2.25, 5.35, 8.45.

LUXOR.—Gene Tierney, Cornel Wilde, **LEAVE HER TO HEAVEN** (A) (Technicolor). FULL SUPPORT.

LYRIC, PARADE.—**SMOKEY** (U) (Technicolor), Fred MacMurray, Anne Baxter; **LUCKY CISCO KID** (A), Cesar Romero.

MAJESTIC, BEARWOOD. — Mon.—Fri. 6, Sat. 5. Barbara Stanwyck, **THE BRIDE WORE BOOTS** (A); also **BIG TOWN** (A).

MAYFAIR — PERRY COMMON. **OLD MOTHER RILEY AT HOME** (A) and **ENCHANTED ISLE**. Thurs.: Courage of Lassie (u).

MAYPOLE, King's Heath. WAR. 2051. Betty Grable, June Haver, in **THE DOLLY SISTERS** (A) (in Technicolor)

NORTHFIELD CINEMA, PRI. 1463. Lee Bowman, **The Walls Came Tumbling Down** (a). **Personality Kid** (u). Thurs.: Claudia and David (a).

OAK, Selly Oak (A.B.C.). SEL. 0139. Bruce Bennett, **TARZAN AND THE GREEN GODDESS** (U); supported by Laurel and Hardy in **JAILBIRDS** (U).

ODEON, BLACKHEATH. BLA. 1036. Janet Blair, **THE MAN AND SPARS** (U) James Craig. **DANGEROUS PARTNERS** (A).

ODEON — KINGSTANDING. **WIFE OF MONTE CRISTO** (A). **JUST WILLIAM** (U). (Last Performance 7.30 p.m)

ODEON, PERRY BARR. BIR. 4455.— **THE PERFECT MARRIAGE** (A) Also **MEN WITH WINGS** (U). Last Complete Performance 7 p.m.

ODEON, SHIRLEY — SHI. 1183. Cont. 2.0 p.m. Johnny Weissmuller, Brenda Joyce, **TARZAN & THE AMAZONS** (U). One Way To Love (u).

ODEON, SUTTON COLDFIELD.— Michael Redgrave, **The Years Between** (a). Last Perf. 7.15. Thurs.: The Perfect Marriage (A)

ODEON — WARLEY David Niven, **THE PERFECT MARRIAGE** (A), 2.15, 5.33, 8.51. Men with Wings (A). Last Perf 7.0.

OLTON CINEMA.—Tom Walls, Glynis Johns, Jeanne de Casalis, **THIS MAN IS MINE** (A). With Full Support.

OLYMPIA, LADYPOOL-RD. VIC. 0124. Ralph Richardson, Edna Best, **SOUTH RIDING** (A). Sidney Toler, **THE JADE MASK** (A).

ORIENT, Aston (A.B.C.). NOR. 1615. Walter Pidgeon, Jane Powell in **HOLIDAY IN MEXICO** (U). Colour. And Full Supporting Programme.

PALACE, Erdington (A.B.C.).' ERD. 1623. Robert Donat, Emlyn Williams, **THE CITADEL** (A) And Full Supporting Programme.

PALLADIUM, Hockley (A.B.C.). NOR. 0380. Karen Morley, Jim Bannon in **THE UNKNOWN** (A). Also **THE MAN WHO DARED** (A).

PAVILION, STIRCHLEY (A.B.C.). KIN. 1241. Walter Pidgeon, Jane Powell, **HOLIDAY IN MEXICO** (U). Colour. And Full Supporting Programme.

PAVILION, Wylde Green (A.B.C.). ERD. 0224. Walter Pidgeon, Jane Powell, **HOLIDAY IN MEXICO** (U). Colour. And Full Supporting Programme.

PICCADILLY, Sparkbrook (A.B.C.). VIC. 1688. Bruce Bennett, **TARZAN AND THE GREEN GODDESS** (U); Laurel and Hardy, **FLYING DEUCES** (A).

PICTURE HOUSE, Aston Cross (A.B.C.). EAS. 0430. Sydney Greenstreet in **THE VERDICT** (A); and also **ONE EXCITING WEEK** (A).

PICTURE HOUSE, Erdington (A.B.C.). ERD. 1484. Edward G. Robinson in **THE STRANGER** (A). Also **RADIO STARS ON PARADE** (A).

PICTURE HOUSE (G.B.). HARBORNE. All Week: David Niven, Kim Hunter, in **A MATTER OF LIFE AND DEATH** (A) (Tech.), the Royal Command Film!

PLAZA, Stockland Green. ERD. 1048. David Niven, **MATTER OF LIFE AND DEATH** (A); **CRIMSON CANARY** (A). Sunday: Behind the Rising Sun (a).

PRINCES, SMETHWICK. SME. 0221. Anna Neagle and Michael Wilding in **PICCADILLY INCIDENT** (A); also **WOMEN IN SPORT** (U).

REGAL, Handsworth (A.B.C.). NOR. 1801. Walter Pidgeon, Jane Powell, **HOLIDAY IN MEXICO**. Colour. And Full Supporting Programme.

RIALTO, HALL GREEN. SPR. 1270. **The Adventures of Robin Hood** (u), Errol Flynn, Olivia de Havilland, Basil Rathbone. Full Support Programme (u)

RINK (G.B.), Smethwick. SME. 0950. Ingrid Bergman, **ADAM HAD FOUR SONS** (A). Free Car Park for Patrons.

RITZ, Bordesley Green (A.B.C.). VIC. 1070. Ida Lupino, Robert Alda in **THE MAN I LOVE** (A); Anne Gwynne, **I RING DOORBELLS** (A).

ROBIN HOOD, Hall Green (A.B.C.). SPR. 2371. Walter Pidgeon, Jane Powell, **HOLIDAY IN MEXICO** (U). (Tech.). Full supporting programme.

ROCK CINEMA, Alum Rock.— Chips Rafferty and Daphne Campbell in **THE OVERLANDERS** (A); **CLUB HAVANA** (A). Thurs.: Carnival (A).

ROYALTY, Harborne (A.B.C.). HAR. 1619. Douglas Fairbanks, **CORSICAN BROTHERS** (A); Dennis O'Keefe, **GETTING GERTIE'S GARTER** (A).

RUBERY CINEMA. Phone 193.—Bela Lugosi, Lon Chaney, in **Frankenstein Meets the Wolf Man** (H); **Easy to Look At** (U). No children under 16 admitted

SAVOY, King's Norton. KIN. 1569.— Alan Ladd, Loretta Young, **AND NOW TO-MORROW** (A); John Carradine in **FACE OF MARBLE** (A).)

SHELDON CINEMA — SHE. 2158. Humphrey Bogart, Lauren Bacall in **THE BIG SLEEP** (A) Thurs.: **CLAUDIA AND DAVID** (A).

SOLIHULL — SOL. 0398 Anthony Hulme and Joy Shelton in **SEND FOR PAUL TEMPLE** (A); **Blossoms in the Dust** (a) Greer Garson

STAR CINEMA, Erdington. EAS. 0461. **SEND FOR PAUL TEMPLE** (A), Anthony Hulme; **Come Out Fighting** (a) East Side Kids. Thurs.: Devotion (u)

TIVOLI PLAYHOUSE, Coventry-road.— **THE PHANTOM** (A) with Tom Tyler. Jeanne Bates; **OUR HEARTS WERE GROWING UP** (A), Gail Russell.

TUDOR, KING'S HEATH (A.B.C.). HIG. 1161. Ida Lupino, Robert Alda, in **THE MAN I LOVE** (A); Anne Crawford in **HEADLINE** (A).

TRIANGLE, Gooch-street, Birmingham. **JUST BEFORE THE DAWN** (A). Warner Baxter; also **HIT THE HAY** (A), Judy Canova.

VICTORIA. EAS 0479. — Paulette Goddard, Ray Milland in **KITTY** (A); **THEY MADE ME A KILLER** (A). Thurs.: G.I. WAR BRIDES (A).

VILLA CROSS (G.B.). NOR. 0607. — The Royal Command Performance Film. David Niven in **A MATTER OF LIFE & DEATH** (A) (Tech.) 3.20, 6.0, 8.35.

WARWICK CINEMA, Acock's Green. Louis Hayward, Joan Bennett, Warren William, Alan Hale in **THE MAN IN THE IRON MASK** (A).

WEOLEY — WEOLEY CASTLE George Raft, Jean Bennett, **The House Across the Bay** (A); **Texas Masquerade** (U). Mon. & Thurs. Cont. from 2.30.

WINDSOR, BEARWOOD. BEA 2244. Mon., Thurs., Sat. from 5. Tues., Wed., Fri. 6. Maureen O'Hara, **Spanish Main** (A); also **Scottish Symphony** (U).

WINSON GREEN. NORTHERN 1790. Her Kind of Man (A), Zachary Scott; **So Dark the Night** (A), Steve Geray. Thurs.: Devotion (U), Ida Lupino.

WEST BROMWICH CINEMAS

CLIFTON, STONE CROSS. STO. 2141. Boris Karloff, Lon Chaney, in **House of Frankenstein** (H). Children under 16 not admitted. **She Wrote the Book** (A)

IMPERIAL, West Bromwich. WES. 0192 David Niven, Kim Hunter, Roger Livesey, **A MATTER OF LIFE AND DEATH** (A) (Tech.), at 3.5, 5.40, 8.20

PALACE CINEMA. WES. 0358.—David Niven, Roger Livesey, **A MATTER OF LIFE & DEATH** (A) (Tech), approx. 2.40, 5.30, 8.15; **Land of the Saints** (u)

PLAZA, WEST BROMWICH. WES. 0030 Fred Astaire and Paulette Goddard in **SECOND CHORUS** (U); also Bill Boyd in **BORDERLAND** (A).

QUEEN'S. WES. 0551. Large Car Park. Paul Lukas and Jane Baxter in **THE CHINESE BUNGALOW** (A); Brian Aherne, **Man Who Lost Himself** (U).

ST. GEORGE'S CINEMA. Phone WES. 0737. Patricia Burke, David Farrar, Richard Tauber, in **THE LISBON STORY** (A).

TOWER (A.B.C.). — WES. 1210. Cary Grant and Alexis Smith in **NIGHT AND DAY** (U). (Tech.). Life Story of Cole Porter.

79

The Lord Mayor, Ald. Albert Bradbeer, receives a greetings scroll, from a German prisoner-of-war, which he will convey to the Lord Mayor of Cologne. Maxstoke P.O.W. Camp, Coleshill, 31st March 1947.

The Chancellor of the Exchequer, Sir Stafford Cripps, meets dignitaries outside St Martin's, 12th May 1947.

The bearded actor, Trevor Howard, is greeted on his arrival, prior to making a personal appearance, at the Gaumont Cinema, Steelhouse Lane, 13th May 1947.

Broad Street, 1947.

e Birmingham Parks Department sets out to improve the lower part of Broad Street, by planting an attractive rock garden in front of the Municipal Bank, 13th May 1947.

Corporation Street, 7th June 1947.

A bit of a snarl-up looks imminent, at the junction of Albert Street and Moor Street, 16th June 1947.

aralysis has eached new peak figure

ATEST Ministry of Health figures, issued esterday, reveal that in-ntile paralysis cases in ngland and Wales eached a peak figure of 2 on September 6.

New notifications in the ain towns were: London, ; Birmingham, 28; Man-ester, 15; Liverpool, 14; underland, Leicester and heffield 10 each; Bradford , Croydon, Ealing, Bristol nd Salford 8 each.

A Ministry of Health offi-al said: "It must be ex-ected that the figures will uctuate for the time be-g.

"This is because the ex-erience of other years howed that the number of ases tends to rise and fall ntermittently until well nto the autumn."

The Ministry state that ne of the greatest single auses of the epidemic preading is the failure of ne general public to wash heir hands.

Local authorities are be-ng urged to provide towels, oap and hot water, free if ossible, in public cloak-ooms.

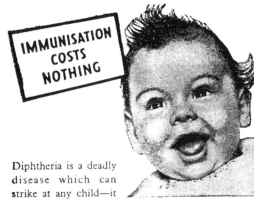

DIPHTHERIA COSTS LIVES

IMMUNISATION COSTS NOTHING

Diphtheria is a deadly disease which can strike at any child—it might be *your* child.

The figures show that a child who has been immunised is much less likely to catch diphtheria, and the chance that he will die from it is 26 times less than that of a child who has not been given protection.

Dare you take this risk? Every baby ought to be protected before he is a year old.

Ask at your Local Council Offices or Welfare Centre for advice.

Issued by the Ministry of Health and the Central Council for Health Education

Adelaide Street/Charles Henry Street, c 1947.

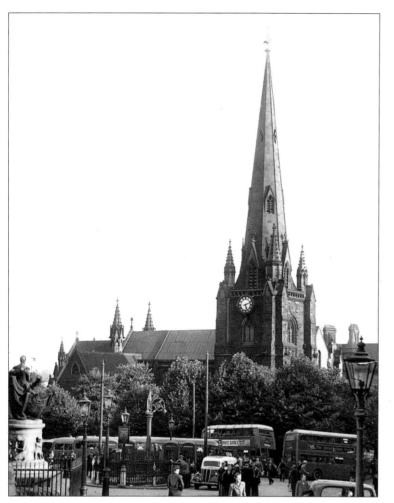

St Martin's, Bull Ring, September 1947.

THIS week the Board of Trade will announce a cut in clothing coupons. At least four coupons are to be deducted from the present allocation of thirty-two, which ends next month.

The shock would have been greater still, the *Sunday Pictorial* was told yesterday, but for the fact that a great proportion of textiles for the next period have already been made up on Utility lines, and are not suitable for export.

By next March most textiles will have been prepared for export, leaving comparatively little for home use. There may, however, be concessions for children's clothing.

Thousands of demobbed Service men and women who are still owed twenty-six clothing coupons by the Board of Trade will get them in November, and details are to be announced next month.

Godfrey Winn, author of "Holiday Camp", surrounded by autograph hunters, at the West End Cinema, 19th September 1947. He was born in Woodbourne Road, Edgbaston.

Edwards Road/Orphanage Road, Erdington, 1947.

Work's convener, Dick Etheridge, addresses a meeting of Austin workers, Longbridge, 1947.

A new sweeper - collector machine, recently put into operation by the Public Works Department of Birmingham Corporation, collects more than a ton of litter per mile, even in suburban districts. Along the Bristol Road, between Priory Road and Oak Tree Lane, four tons 5cwt. of rubbish was collected on one trip.

Birmingham Corporation's salvage department daily screens the city's waste for recoverable materials, and the war-time scheme is still in operation for the collection of waste paper—which should be put out for the dustmen in separate packages. Private enterprise, too, works effectively to collect waste paper for re-pulping.

B'HAM AGAIN LEADS

With a total of all categories of 5,286 houses built up to the end of August, Birmingham once more leads the county boroughs listed in the Ministry of Health's latest returns issued to-day. Coventry, with 2,515, drops to sixth place.

Birmingham's total is made up of 932 new houses completed since the war under the Corporation's schemes, with 222 rebuilt war-destroyed homes and 2,763 temporary houses provided by the Ministry of Works. Private enterprise was responsible for 951 new houses and 418 rebuilds. These figures give a total for the Corporation of 1,154 and 1,369 for private enterprise.

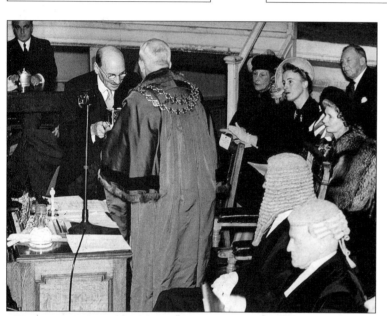

The Prime Minister, the Rt. Hon. Clement Attlee, receives the Freedom of the city, Town Hall, 18th October 1947.

Bull Street, October 1947.

John Cheesman (right) and Robin Clarke, both originally enrolled as Bevin Boys, Jubilee Colliery, Hamstead, c 1947.

Jubilee Colliery Mine's Rescue Team, on a training course, in Dudley, 1947. The two men, not kitted up, are their instructors.

CITY OF BIRMINGHAM   CONSUMER'S COPY **2A**

COAL DISTRIBUTION ORDER, 1943

NOTIFICATION OF REGISTRATION OF CONTROLLED PREMISES WITH A
LICENSED MERCHANT

To   Mr. E. Broadbent.,

Plot 4, Colleen Avenue,   Date 22nd Oct. 1947.

off Peplins Way., Kings Norton. 30.

BIRMINGHAM

I hereby notify you that your registration with the undermentioned merchant in respect of fuel supplies to the above premises has been duly completed.   Depot:- Kings Norton.

A copy of this notice has been forwarded to your registered merchant :—

Messrs A. E. Richardson.,

167, Park Rd., Hockley,   (725)

Birmingham.18.

You must purchase all your fuel requirements from your registered merchant unless permission to transfer registration has been granted by the Local Fuel Overseer. Failure to observe these provisions renders you liable to penalties under the Defence Regulations.

CIVIC CENTRE,   A. E. GILBERT,
BIRMINGHAM, 1   Examined by   Local Fuel Overseer.

P466—85—E

The crowds leave Bromford Races, c 1947.

PRINCESS'S THANKS TO BIRMINGHAM

The Lord Mayor of Birmingham has received the following letter of thanks signed by Princess Elizabeth:

BUCKINGHAM PALACE,
16th November, 1947.

My Lord Mayor.

The magnificent silver tea service which the City of Birmingham has sent me is an object of admiration to all who have seen it, and it would be difficult for me to exaggerate the pleasure which this Wedding Present has given me.

The world wide reputation for silver which Birmingham has long enjoyed is certainly upheld in this service, and I can assure you that Lieutenant Mountbatten and I are delighted with it.

Whenever we use it, which will be often, it will remind us of the generosity of the people of Birmingham and of the good wishes which we know that they send us at this very happy period in our lives.

Yours sincerely,
(Signed) ELIZABETH.

New Street, looking across to High Street, 1947.

Albert Place, Friston Street, Ladywood, December 1947.

710 Coventry Road, Small Heath, 2nd December 1947.

Rear of Hospital Street, Hockley, 9th December 1947.

The Lord Mayor, Coun. John Burman, pays a visit to the ex-servicemen's canteen, Windmill Street,
8th December 1947.

On Air Force leave, Norman Bailey
dances with his sister, Lily, Tower
Ballroom, December 1947.

Last minute shopping in the Bull Ring, Christmas Eve 1947.

Bridge players, involved in the International Tournament, meet the Lord Mayor and Lady Mayoress, Coun. and Mrs John Burman, and their daughter, Rosanne, 28th February 1948.

Hospital Street, Hockley, 1948.

Macdonald Street, Highgate, February 1948.

The retiring Midland Regional Director of the BBC, Percy Edgar, is presented with a motor lawn mower at the BBC Club, Broad Street, 8th April 1948. He was known to a generation of listening children as "Uncle Percy".

Vic Oliver, usually seen as a comedian and violinist, conducts the British Concert Orchestra, Hippodrome, 25th April 1948.

THESE are a few of the many handsome postage stamps issued in the Commonwealth and Empire during the past two years. Unfortunately we cannot show them in their full colours, as this is not allowed by the G.P.O. The Hong Kong Victory issue (29-8-46) is brown and red : that of Malta (8-6-46) is blue, as are the Jamaica (20-8-46) and Barbados (1-4-47) issues. Of the three Royal Visit issues, that of Southern Rhodesia (1-4-47) is scarlet and black ; Swaziland (17-2-47) scarlet ; and South Africa (17-2-47) blue. The New Zealand Health issue (24-10-46) is green and orange-brown ; the Australian Mitchell Centenary (14-10-46) grey-olive ; the Falkland Is. (10-12-46) scarlet and black ; and the Dependencies (11-2-46) black and claret.

Barrow's Self-Service Restaurant, Corporation Street, 1948.

Barrow's Despatch Warehouse, Dalton Street, 1948.

Spiceal Street, 1948.

The King and Queen visit the British Industries Fair, Castle Bromwich, 11th May 1948...

... and on to examine a patent food container...

… and finally to the ICI stand for another demonstration.

The King and Queen meet some of the children and wounded ex-servicemen, outside the Town Hall,
11th May 1948.

The King and Queen's departure from the Council House, 11th May 1948.

The crowds converge on the Royal cavalcade as it travels slowly along Corporation Street, 11th May 1948.

Dame Elizabeth Cadbury with the May Queen, Jean Ridgewell, Bournville fete, 1948.

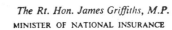

The Rt. Hon. James Griffiths, M.P.
MINISTER OF NATIONAL INSURANCE

THE 5th July 1948 will be a great day in the development of our British Social Services. On that day we shall see National Insurance, including Industrial Injury Insurance, in full operation, supporting—and supported by—Family Allowances, the National Health Service and National Assistance. We have indeed come a long way from the Old Age Pensions Act of 1908 (which gave the 5s. a week pension at 70), to this new system of Social Security which provides help for childbirth, in sickness, in unemployment, in bereavement, and in old age.

The system will provide for everybody without exception: men, women and children, young and old, rich and poor, married and single, employer and employed, those working on their own account, and those not working at all.

This booklet tells you how much you must pay each week and what benefits you will receive in return. It is not possible, of course, to set out all the details in such a short guide, and I am afraid you will find some parts complicated, and perhaps difficult to apply to yourself. If you are in doubt on any point please ask your nearest National Insurance Office for help. You will find the staff there very ready to give you all the help and explanation they can.

The success of this great Insurance Scheme depends upon the willing co-operation of every one of us. Our benefits must be paid for out of our contributions and our taxes. This scheme is, therefore, more than an Act of Parliament; it is an act of faith in the British people. That faith, I know, is not misplaced.

James Griffiths

THEATRE ROYAL

Phone MIDLAND 1355-6-7 · BIRMINGHAM · Proprietors · Moss Empires Ltd.

Managing Director · Val Parnell · Chairman · Prince Littler · Manager · C. J. Price

Commencing MONDAY, MAY 23rd · FOR TWO WEEKS
EVENINGS at 7 p.m.
MATINEES · THURSDAYS and SATURDAYS at 2.30

BERNARD DELFONT and BEN KANTER
by arrangement with HANS BARTSCHI
PRESENT

AN ENTIRELY NEW STREAMLINED VERSION OF
OSCAR STRAUS'
MERRY MUSICAL
A GLITTERING & LAVISH
Production with a Thousand Laughs

The
CHOCOLATE SOLDIER

PRODUCED BY
RICHARD BIRD

**JESSICA JAMES
ROY ROYSTON
ERIC STARLING
BEVERLEY WRIGHT**
GORDON NEEDHAM
GENE MARIAN
PRUDENCE HYMAN
GEORGE GERHARDT
AND
FRED EMNEY

FULL CHORUS & ORCHESTRA UNDER THE DIRECTION OF JAN HURST

NEW LYRICS!
By HAROLD PURCELL
NEW DECOR!
By CHARLES READING
NEW COSTUMES!
by R. St JOHN ROPER
NEW DANCES!
By LYDIA SOKOLOVA

FRED EMNEY

REVISED BOOK BY GUY BOLTON

Martineau Street/Bull Street, June 1948.

99

White Hart, Tile Cross Road, c 1948.

Joan McFarland (left) and friend, successfully
recovering from TB, West Heath Sanatorium,
1948. Yes, you are right about those banjoes!

A group of Midlanders, including several people from Birmingham,
at an agricultural camp at Yeovil, Summer 1948.

Corporation Street, 14th July 1948.

Limberlost Tennis Club, Handsworth Wood,
c 1948.

Yardley Road, Acocks Green, c 1948.

Ald. Albert Bradbeer opens the Mobile Safety First
Exhibition, Civic Centre, 16th August 1948.

Great Francis Street/Clarendon Street, Vauxhall, c 1948.

Camp Hill, 1948.

Thomas Street/Adelaide Street/Macdonald Street, Highgate, 1948.

Co-op Dairy Manager, Mr Procter, (second right) presents a cheque to Eric Hollies, as a result of the Benefit Match. 10th September 1948. The Warwickshire captain, Tom Dollery, is on the left.

Phone
BEArwood 2880.

155, POPLAR AVENUE,
EDGBASTON,
BIRMINGHAM 17.

Sept 15th 1948

Statement of Fees

To **NEVILLE RAYNER,**

MUS. BAC.

Pianoforte Playing	Elementary	3 gns
	Moderate	3½ gns
	Advanced	4 gns
Harmony etc.	And all	
Exam. Coaching	Theoretical Subjects	3 gns.
Music		

Total £ _____

For a Term of 10 lessons ~~beginning~~ *over a 12 weekly period.*
ALL FEES PAYABLE IN ADVANCE.

St Martin's Church, from Moat Row, 29th November 1948.

Staff party, Royalty Cinema, High Street, Harborne, Christmas 1948.

Gothic Arcade, Snow Hill, c 1949.

A temporary car park, opposite the Odeon, New Street, January 1949.

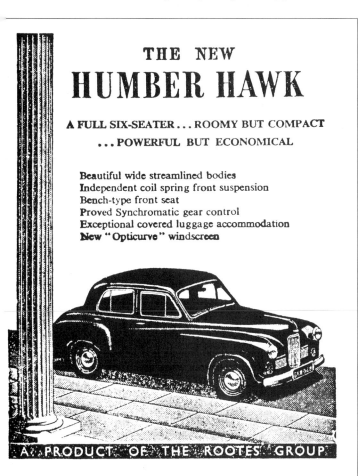

THE NEW

HUMBER HAWK

**A FULL SIX-SEATER . . . ROOMY BUT COMPACT
. . . POWERFUL BUT ECONOMICAL**

Beautiful wide streamlined bodies
Independent coil spring front suspension
Bench-type front seat
Proved Synchromatic gear control
Exceptional covered luggage accommodation
New "Opticurve" windscreen

A PRODUCT OF THE ROOTES GROUP

HARBORNE MOTORS
YORK STREET, HARBORNE
Phone : 3056

Mrs Florence Thursfield in the kitchen of her
home in Brunswick Road, Handsworth, c 1949.
If you needed a single image, to best represent
domestic life in the forties, this would have
to be a contender.

A happy example of co-operation between management and workers comes to-day from the Cyclo Gear Company, of Potters Hill, Aston—where the above picture was taken—75 per cent. of whose output of cycle gears and cycle accessories is exported to 55 different countries. Te 120 men and 130 women employed by this firm are working voluntaily a 62½-hour week instead of the usual 47½-hour week, and at normal piecework rates. It was their own idea to help with a very full order book. "It involves starting at 7.30 a.m. and finishing at 8 p.m.," said Mr. Edwin Camillis, the firm's works manager. "It means, of course, that we can get bigger production for the same overheads." Despite increased prices of raw materials, and other higher costs, the firm, by means of co-operation with the workers and bigger outputs, has contrived to keep the prices of its goods down to the 1942 level.

Toolroom, Cyclo Gear Co. Ltd., Aston, 1949.

Icknield Street, looking towards Warstone Lane, 4th February 1949.

The Birmingham Eagles Roller Speed Skating Club, Embassy Sportsdrome, Walford Road, Sparkhill, 1949.

Operatic singer and actor, Paul Robeson, acknowledges the welcome from the waiting crowd, Town Hall, 25th February 1949.

Cadbury Bros. Ltd., Bournville, February 1949.

Charter Rates:

6 Passenger Twin Engine Machines **2/6** per mile
3   ,,   Machines - - **1/6** ,,
2   ,,   ,,   - - **1/-** ,,

*These rates are NOT per person
but for the whole Aircraft in each case*

WINGED FEET
direct to Paris
from Birmingham

in a famous Douglas D.C.3 aircraft; thence to the Riviera, Corsica, Italy, Spain, Majorca or Switzerland. Ask your Travel Agent for details of Air France services from Birmingham, London, Manchester, Glasgow and Belfast.

Return fare Birmingham - Paris £13.0.0

AIR FRANCE

ELMDON AIRPORT, BIRMINGHAM.   SHELDON 2441

Lord Pakenham, Minister of Civil Aviation, prepares to open the first international service from Birmingham by BEA, to Paris, 8th April 1949. He is now known as Lord Longford.

Sutherland Street, Aston, 1949.

Navigation Street, c 1949.

Navigation Street/Hill Street, 12th April 1949.

The junction of Suffolk Street and John Bright Street, 1949.

Proving once again the popularity of Royal visits,
as the crowds turn out to greet Princess Elizabeth and the
Duke of Edinburgh, Victoria Square, 10th May 1949.

The Firm have engaged for the Cadbury programme Britain's No. 1 film star, John Mills. Each Sunday night from 9.30 to 10 p.m. he broadcasts a programme called "A Goodnight Story," in which the works of famous short

John Mills at the microphone

story writers are presented in dramatised form. The following are among the well-known works already broadcast: *The Purple Pileus* (H. G. Wells), *Family Cares* (W. W. Jacobs), *Sire de Maletroit* (R. L. Stevenson), *The Kite* (Somerset Maugham), *The White Pony* (H. E. Bates) and *The Canterville Ghost* (Oscar Wilde).

The growing popularity of John Mills and the Cadbury programme is very evident from the ever-increasing fan-mail which arrives at Bournville each week.

Many people in the Birmingham area find it difficult to get first-class reception from Luxembourg, but the transmitter strength is rapidly improving. We recommend "A Goodnight Story" as a very pleasant entertainment to round off Sunday's listening. It advertises Bourn-vita as the "goodnight" food drink.

Luxembourg's wave length is 1,293 metres.

Heneage Street, Aston, 1949.

Harborne Lane, Harborne, May 1949.

FINAL LEAGUE POSITIONS 1948-49

LEAGUE I

	Pld.	Won	Drn.	Lost	GOALS For	Agst.	Pts.
Portsmouth	42	25	8	9	84	42	58
Manchester United	42	21	11	10	77	44	53
Derby County	42	22	9	11	74	55	53
Newcastle United	42	20	12	10	70	56	52
Arsenal	42	18	13	11	74	44	49
Wolver'ton Wanderers	42	17	12	13	79	66	46
Manchester City	42	15	15	12	47	51	45
Sunderland	42	13	17	12	49	58	43
Charlton	42	15	12	15	63	67	42
Aston Villa	42	16	10	16	60	76	42
Stoke	42	16	9	17	66	68	41
Liverpool	42	13	14	15	53	43	40
Chelsea	42	12	14	16	69	68	38
Burnley	42	12	14	15	43	50	38
Bolton Wanderers	42	14	10	18	59	68	38
Blackpool	42	11	16	15	54	67	38
Birmingham City	42	11	15	16	36	38	37
Everton	42	13	11	18	41	63	37
Middlesbrough	42	11	12	19	46	57	34
Huddersfield	42	12	10	20	40	69	34
Preston	42	11	11	20	62	75	33
Sheffield United	42	11	11	20	57	78	33

The first bus to be painted in the new British Railway colours 12th May 1949. It was to convey relief train crews from Saltley various local stations.

Midland Red Beauty Queen, Rosalind Allen, with her ladies-in-waiting and the competition judges, at the Annual Sports' Day, 5th July 1949.

Easy Row, 1949.

Benson Road Elementary School, Soho, c 1949.

Dr G.T. Warwick (2nd right) and a party of geography students from the University of Birmingham, on expedition to the Arctic Circle of Norway, 1949.

Contestants from Turves Green Secondary Modern School prepare to leave, from New Street Station, for Stockholm, to represent England in the world gymnastics' festival, July 1949.

No parking problems for the Bond car, Waterloo Street, 1949.

Monument Road/Reservoir Road, Ladywood, September 1949.

Palais de Danse, Monument Road, Edgbaston, c 1949.

Oaktree Lane/Bristol Road, Selly Oak, 1949.

Chamberlain Square, 23rd September 1949.

Montgomery Street, Small Heath,
23rd November 1949.

War-damaged furniture at Cambridge Street stores,
1949.

AL SHARKEY FORMS OWN QUARTET

Appearing each Wednesday and
Saturday at the Moorpool Ballroom, Harborne, is a quartet led
by trumpeter Al Sharkey, who
recently left Musical Direction
(Vincent Ladbrook's office) to
launch out as a leader in his own
right.

Pamela Venn now with Sonny Rose

Nineteen-year-old Pamela Venn,
now singing with Sonny Rose
and his Band at the West End
Ballroom, Birmingham, began her
career as a vocalist at the age of
14. She was introduced in
"Opportunity Knocks" by
Birmingham University bandleader Allan Ayres in June last.

Carol Service, St Martin's Church,
22nd December 1949.

Bordesley Street, 30th December 1949.

Back Cover: Louis de Camillis, the founder of Cyclo Gear Co. Ltd., of Aston, complete with gas mask, Barr Beacon, April 1941. This might be a good idea for cyclists today, to combat pollution!

ACKNOWLEDGEMENTS

(for providing photographs, for encouragement and numerous other favours)

Norman Bailey; The late Dorothy Bevan; The Birmingham City Council Dept. of Planning and Architecture; Birmingham International Airport; The Birmingham Post and Mail Ltd.; Hilda Broadbent; Anne Cannell; Dave and Kath Carpenter; John Cheesman; Annette Dickers; Eddystone Radio Ltd.; John Enticknap; Peter Fletcher; Joyce Gill; Robin and Elaine Harriott; George and Jeanette Holt; John Hotchkiss; The International Print Shop (Kings Norton Green); Anne Jennings; Thelma Jones; Jim Kendall; Joyce Lockwood; Millie Mills; Dennis Moore; George Peace; David Perrins; Rex Preece; Douglas Price; Clyde Riley; Travel West Midlands; The University of Birmingham; Andy Wade; Joan Wanty; Joan Ward; Ron While; Rosemary Wilkes.

Please forgive any possible omissions. Every effort has been made to include all organisations and individuals involved in the book.

Princess Elizabeth and the Duke of Edinburgh receive a regal bow from Michael Burman, Stechford Station, 10th May 1949.